St. Paul's

Journeys to Greece and Cyprus

St. Paul's
Journeys to Greece and Cyprus

by
ATHAN. J. DELICOSTOPOULOS
ph. D., D. D.
Formerly Professor at the University of Athens

**With the latest
archaelogical, historic, cultural and tourist
information**

ATHENS 1995

Efstathiadis Group S.A.
Agiou Athanasiou Street,
GR - 145 65 Anixi, Attikis

ISBN 960 226 386 5

© Efstathiadis Group A.E. 1995

Printed and bound in Greece by Efstathiadis Group S.A.

This book is dedicated
TO THOSE

interested in retracing the steps
of St. Paul through the ancient biblical
sites of Greece and Cyprus.

The author

To the Visitor

You have entered into Greece, the country of myth and magic. This can be an entrancing experience. The travel agency may have fixed your route, but something of your inner self has helped to select the experience.

This country of spirit and light can occasion not only relaxation, but regeneration: a re-birth. A journey can alter people. Travelling can be the beginning of a spiritual journey. Geothe experienced this. The same can happen to each of us.

It is immaterial whether this is your first journey into this country which has been tilled by the Greek spirit and cultivated by the Word of God. What is of import is that the land you are stepping on was crossed with respect and awe, by another traveller, St. Paul, the man who came and planted in the waiting land the tree of love, the spiritual sapling of the leader of the biggest movement of all time.

This small book will guide your steps in this land of genius. The work of the Apostle of the nations is explained simply. This book restricts itself to Paul's travels in Greece and Cyprus.*

St. Paul's example can be followed by all of us. He believed in something passionately. He evaluated its worth and spent his most valuable asset, his life, in spreading the word of hope and salvation. Myriads heard his message; innumerable thousands accepted the life of love. Paul was not alone. Beside him was always the One, He for whom he spoke and fought, the Unique, Christ our Lord.

Today, you, travelling around the places Paul visited, can discover all that science-history, archeology, philology, theology and philosophy- has to offer you about the man who worked to change the destiny of Greece, Europe and the whole western world.

* Asia Minor and Italy may be covered in a companion volume.

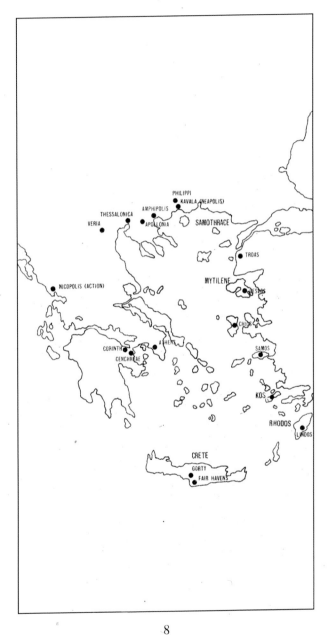

Paul's proclamation sounds across the centuries. "There is neither Jew nor Greek, there is neither slave nor free, there is neither male nor female; for your are all one in Jesus Christ." (St. Paul's Epistle to the Galatians 3, 28)

If you are in Athens on the afternoon of the 29th of June and you walk to the Areopagus you may attend a solemn ceremony. It is a special vesper of the Holiday of St. Peter and St. Paul. The vesper is sung near the Acropolis that outstanding monument of Greek genius.

Every summer on the same day, at the same time and at the same place the words of the address of St. Paul to the Athenians are read as they were spoken by him. (Acts of the Apostles 17, 19-32).

As long as this country of ours remains free, the same holy text will be read by a humble priest in the heat of the warm summer afternoon. It is a continuing reminder to Greeks and visitors alike of how the Greeks of classical antiquity learned to accept the Christian way of life, of thought and of hope.

This is the debt Greece owes to St. Paul.

Athan. J. Delicostopoulos Ph. D., D.D.
Formerly Professor at the University of Athens.

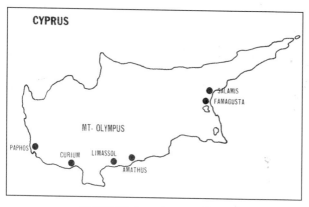

St. Paul's Missionary Journey to Cyprus
(Part of the First Missionary Journey)

9

PART ONE

The Historic Background of the Time of St. Paul(*).

Only a few years separate the birth of Paul and Christ's incarnation. The One, the Unique, was born in the cave of Bethlehem, the other, the first after the One, was born in the cosmopolitan city of Tarsus, near the wild mountain of Taurus.

When Paul was born, Tarsus was a large city and centre of communications, the boundary of two civilizations: the Greek-Roman of the West and the Semite-Babylonian of the East. Tarsus was a busy commercial city, a centre of international trade. It was also a centre of culture and education. Furthermore it was a historic city. River Cydnus was navigable and connected the city with the sea. The sea became the element of life for the Apostle, simultaneously creative and dangerous. Cydnus was the river up which Cleopatra had sailed to captivate Mark Antony in 41 B.C., which episode Shakespear made immortal in paraphrasing Plutarch, the Greek biographer and moralist.

According to history and to local tradition Alexander the Great, the king of Macedonia and conqueror of the world had encamped near the waterfall of the big city, having crossed the Cilician Gates in chasing Darius, the king of Persians. Tired as he was, Alexander dived into the waters of the river, icy from the melting snows of Taurus. The result was that the great hero became sick and was lying in bed, his temperature having risen dangerously. Philip, the physician, the pupil of Hippocrates,

(*) This book has been written on the basis of wide bibliography published in most European languages. It is the result of scientific research work. Since its aim is to inform visitors to Greece and Cyprus of the journeys of St. Paul in these two countries and to give the archaeological, historic cultural and general background, plus modern tourist information in detail, no reference is made through footnotes to the various sources, The only reference that is made is to the New Testament.

saved the king's life by giving him a drug. Parmenion, one of the generals of the king, had sent a written message to the sick king warning him that the doctor had been bribed by Darius so that he might poison Alexander. Alexander, quick in thought and decision, with one hand took the cup and drank the medicine while with the other hand he gave the letter of Parmenion to his doctor. The trust and belief of the king in his physician, and his magnanimity, courage and boldness in facing death, saved the king's life. If Alexander's life had not been saved at that time, history certainly would have taken another derection. The Est-Hellenic civilizatin, which prepared the road for the coming of Christianity could not have been a reality.

But one may ask: How is this episode related to Paul? Looking at history from the vantage point of time, one can see the relation. The saving of the life of Alexander the Great took place in Tarsus. In the same place Paul was born, the man who, redeeming himself with the boldness of belief, went around the world teaching taht belief is the best and most effective medicine for salvation. This is the connection between two historic facts.

When in the thirtieth year of the monarchy of Augustus, the incarnation of God took place in Palestine, most of the known cities of the world were Greek and their countries were being hellenised. It was three and a half centuries earlier that the genius of Alexander the Great had hoisted the flag of Hellenism and had dashed from Macedonia through the Hellespont to conquer the countries of the East. Now, Christianity, armed with the panoply of the Greek language, Greek thought and Greek political organization, dashed from Palestine to Europe aiming at conquering its countries and its spirit. What Alexander the Great did in one direction, the same exactly was done by Paul in the opposite. Two magnificent movements for the salvation of the world, for the advancement of civilization, for the attainment of happiness in the struggle for amelioration.

Many were the factors that contributed to the triumph of Christianity. First was the perfection fo faith, the revealed ful-

Athens: St. Paul. A mosaic in the church of St. Dionysios the Areopagite on Skoufa Street, Kolonaki.

ness of truth, which was sanctioned by the sacrifice at Calvary. Then follow other factors most important of which was that due to the struggle between philosophy and the various religions, the ancient doctrines had become atrophied and society, especially that of the intellectuals, had become devoid of any faith. Furthermore the conquest of the world by the Greeks caused the amalgamation of various deities and prepared human thinking for the understanding and for the acceptance of the one God. The hellenisation of the world helped greatly to build the avenue down which Christianity was destined to march.

The Greek language and the Greek political organization helped towards that end. Greek language, with its perfection and its possibilities to express the highest of ideas and thoughts, was the perfect instrument. This instrument was used by all social strata, by the nobility and by the working class. The Greek political organization was used as the model of the first christian communities. Beyong these, the Roman conquest of the world contributed also to the triumph of Christianity. The world was in need of intellectual, moral and social reformation. This could not be done unless the barriers that kept the nations divided were thrown down. Rome contributed to advancement of Christianity through the political unity to which it subjected the countries occupied by its armies at that time.

The political unity of the world, however, was prepared by the Greek conquest. The administrative, military, numusmatic, judicial, political and most of all intellectual and linguistic unity prevailed also in the states that were created after the death of Alexander the Great. This multiple unity was in need of a roof, which was offered by Rome. No one can deny, however, that all moral elements of that political unity were the products of the previous fights of Hellenism. It was Hellenism that united the nations and the peoples and made them more receptive towards the innovations of Christianity.

The Greek language was the direct instrument for the preaching, for the interpretation and for the expansion of the religion. The Greek language was spoken from one end to the other of the Roman empire. Trade too, a most powerful factor of development, was conducted in the Greek language, even by the Jews. All these factors combined to make the Greek language a ready vehicle for the spirit of God. Paul's knowledge of the Greek language became the instrument of his preaching of the truth. This preparation, however, in no way means that the people did not oppose Jesus, his teachings and Paul as well. The enmity expressed towards Christianity contributed, in a paradoxical way, to its expansion.

The world owes much to Paul. The appearance of the "man of Macedonia" in Paul's vision at the Troas and Paul's crossing from Asia Minor to Europe characterize the beginning of a tremendous spiritual event, which not only shook those times, but changed the history of the world. History is first a matter of spiritual and philosophic conquest and second of territorial occupations.

St. Paul's Origin

To-day science knows much about Paul, but the Bible is the basic source from which we draw information and vital elements about him, his ministry and his missionary activities. Thirteen Epistles bearing his name as their author were handed down through the centuries to us. The Acts of the Apostles, written by St. Luke, the physician and fellow traveller of Paul, complete the historic picture.

The author, in this book, has avoided too deep an involvement in the scientific side of presenting St. Paul. The book aims at guiding tourists and interested visitors in tracing the steps of St. Paul through Greece and Cyprus, and in interpreting the spiritual past as it is preserved in ancient biblical sites today.

Five of the thirteen Epistles of Paul were addressed to churches in Greece: two to the Corinthians, two to the Thessalonians and one to the Philippians. All these five Epistles are of great interest to us, since they deal directly with Paul's journeys to Greece. The other letters are of great importance to us too, especially the long ones, the one to the Romans and that to the Galatians. By using Paul's letters to the Christian communities we learn about the churches that he established, about Paul's faith, ideas and the dialectic power of the eloquent orator as well as about his feelings, his character and his whole personality.

In spite of the facts that the Acts of the Apostles are a source of a lesser importance, in comparison to the Epistles, we do rely on them since they give us material and imformation of great value. The author of the Acts writes on the basis of his personal experiences or draws information form eye witnesses of the deeds Paul, of his life and missionary activities, starting with the vision on the road to Damascus, the moment when the conversion and the call of the great Apostle took place. It was at that moment that the new religion won the strongest personality on earth, the most active messenger of the power of God, the prototype of the world's converts, the man who became a heroic figure, towering above priests, officers, governors and kings.

Neither the Epistles nor the Acts of the Apostles give us any information about Paul's years of youth and his martyrdom. What we know about his death comes form the letter of Clemens, Bishop of Rome, to the Corinthians. This letter was written at the end of the first century or at the beginning of the second. We find in this letter a brief account of the life of the Apostle. He was imprisoned seven times. He was saved by escaping. He was stoned. He travelled to the end of the Western world, that is to Spain. He preached the doctrines of Jesus in front of authorities, governors and kings and finally he died for what he believed in.

Paul was born at the beginning of the first century in Tarsus and died in Rome in A.D. 67. In his letter to Philemon, which he wrote between the years 58 and 62, he calls himself "πϱεσβύτην" i.e. an old man (cf. Philemon 9). The criteria by which one may call oneself an old man vary, but if one takes into consideration the average length of human life in Paul's time, then the characterisation is fully justified. At the stoning of Stephen, Paul, under his Hebrew name Saul, is mentioned as "neanias", i.e. young man (Acts 7,58). Stephens's death took place in A.D. 33 or 34. One can easily conclude that then Paul was about 25 years old.

"I am a Jew, born at Tarsus in Cilicia" (Acts 22,3). This is the identity that Paul presented to the Roman tribune in Jerusalem upon his arrest, when they inquired who he was and what he had done. The man, who did not make a distinction between a Jew and a Gentile, between a Greek and a Barbarian, was not brought up among the idyllic hills of Galilee, but in a rich commercial city, in a busy trading centre, whose citizens travelled far and wide and where one could find mixed all the races of the Roman Empire. The Hellenistic influence on Paul is obvious. The atmosphere of Tarsus, where Paul grew up and spent many years of his life even after his conversion testifies to this fact. The Jews of the diaspora (by the time of Paul they must have numbered four and one half million, if not more; that is six per cent of the total population of the empire), living in a city like Tarsus, could not escape from this Hellenistic influence in school as well as in life. Science to-day admits that the Greek way of life and thought have exercised a strong influence on Paul. He must have lived in Tarsus for years. There is no doubt that Paul was proficient in Greek, both in speaking and in writing. Greek for him was a second mother tongue.

"I am from Tarsus, a citizen of no mean city" (Acts 21,39). Paul indeed was very pround of his city. He was justified in this. Tarsus a Hellenistic city, was competing with Alexandria and Athens for priority in education. One should not forget that in great cities like Tarsus, Ephesus, Pergamum and Petra, Greek civilization flourished. It was in Ionia, that philosophy had its birth, long beforeit illuminated the city of Athens. It was there, across the Aegean Sea, on the coast of Asia Minor that men first discarded the idea of myth and asked in an epistemological way about the truth.

Rome was taking the paedagogues for its princes from Tarsus. It was in Tarsus that the Greek intellect and the Greek language, the Roman law and Jewish austerity, the Greek way of life, the athletic spirit, the commercial genius, the oriental magic and the occult religions co-existed and commingled. Paul grew up in the atmosphere of the Greek "polis" (city-state), that unique colonialinstrument on which Alexander the Great based his grandiose plan for the conquest of the East and its impregnation with the genuine Greek spirit. Paul's environment was characterized by Greek education and culture, the universal Greek language and the Greek communal life.

Paul was a Roman citizen. He was proud of being a "civis romanus". He emphasizes it on several occasions. There were times that Roman citizenship saved his life. Paul's family had acquired Roman citizenship in Tarsus. In this great cosmopolitan city there was never strict distinction between the Gentiles and the Jews. Those of the Jews who were in a position to pay a certain amount of money could acquire Roman citizenship and could take part in the administration of the city.

The fact that Paul did not come form the ghetto, the section of the city in which many Jews lived and grew up, explains the extensiveness of his mind, his liberal attitude towards the Gentiles, and his disciplined behaviour towards the state and the authorities which helps him find friendly words, even praying to God for "those in power and in office".

The Roman citizen belonged to the lower class of the Roman nobility and bore the name and surname of his protector, to whom he owned the acquisition of his Roman citizenship, e.g. Claudius Antonius. One should notice, however, that in Greek citiers the Roman citizens were never referred with their surnames. Paul, for his compatriots was only Paulus. Saul, his sacred Hebrew name was used only by his family at home as was customary with the Jews of the diaspora.

Whatever God has given to man as natural gift, whatever education and culture has added to it, can be purified by the Spirit of God and be used as constructive elements for a higher, spiritual world. Looking in amazements at the great life of Paul, we can only stand and admire the way in which nature and divine grace are linked to each other and itnerweave one of the most successful human careers, tragic but glorious. Tarsus gave birth to the man who would inherit the testament of Alexander the Great for the unification of East and West.

Paul's Studies

Paul's education and studies were the most thorough that the son of a rich Jew merchant of the diaspora could follow. His father was a Pharisee. The Pharisees believed passionately in being separate, which is what exactly the word Pharisee means.

He was a man of austere national and religious principles. He initiated his son into the sacred language of the original text of the Bible. He brought up his son as a strict Jew, a Pharisee.

At school Paul's vernacular was Hellenistic Greek. It was there that Paul studied the Bible in the standard Greek version, the Septuagint, made in Alexandria between 287 and 284 B.C. At home Paul's family spoke Greek. One however should notice that the Jews of that time had a very successful educational system.

Paul, at six years of age, started attending the school of the synagogue. The Greek boys of the same age, could face their Jewish playmates with a certain contempt, but young Paul knew that he belonged to a people that had had a glorious history as a nation.

The second stage of Paul's education started when he became ten years old. This stage was not as happy as the previous one. At this age the young Jew started learning the "oral law", as they called it. That is a whole series of new definitions of sins. According to the rabbis these new prohibitins were obligatory like the ten commandments. The imposition of the oral law exercised a negative influence on the fine, sensitive heart of young Paul, who was living in an entirely different, bright and civilized world. Certainly the laws would have caused dangerous feelings of reaction in Paul. The splendid years of youth and its paradise were overshadowed by the "oral law" and its long list of "sins".

We can imagine Paul's father as very serious, silent, just and introverted man, who every Saturday walked quietly to the Synagogue. He would not spare the rod in dealing with young Paul's character as it was before Paul's conversion, till the moment that Paul was, by the grace of God, transformed into Paul the Apostle. Perhaps young Paul needed the rod of we think of the wild and turbulent spirit of the persecutor if the Christians. Paul would have been perhaps a stubborn and a very difficult child to manage. Later when he was writing his letter to the Ephesians, he insisted in the paedagogical advice: "Fathers, do not provoke your children to anger, but bring them up the discipline and instruction of the Lord" (Eph. 6,5). In writing this he had in mind his father and all his austerity.

The generation gap is not only a present day problem. There have always been tyrannical fathers and touchy children, oldfashioned parents and youth of modern ideas. We possess no information about Paul's brothers. We know, however, that Paul had a sister who later appears to have lived as a married woman in Jerusalem (Acts 23,16). It would have been very interesting to know about Paul's mother. Paul never mentions anything about her. Possibly she died early and Paul grew up without his mother's love. This could be an explanation for why Paul was so appreciative of the mother of Rufus, whom he called and respected as his mother too. (Rom. 16,13).

According to Strabo, Tarsus, at the time of Paul, was superior to Alexandria and to Athens as an educational centre. The philosophy of the Stoics flourished. The city was a stoic stronghold. Antinodoros was the best known stoic philospher teaching there. Augustus himself had been a pupil of a Tarsian stoic. Later on, in discussing Paul's address at the Areopague in Athens, we will see him confronting Athenian Stoicism. Paul was a Semite. Zeno of Kitium (Cyprus) the great teacher and founder of Stoicism was not a Greek but a Semite like Paul. We can not here totally evaluate the influence that Tarsian Stoicism might have exercised upon Paul.

One thing is certain, however, Paul learned Greek in Tarsus and there he came in direct contact with the Hellenic way of life and thought. Furthermore, Paul was brought up in the pious circle of the local synagogue. It was in Tarsian synagogue that Paul was taught to observe the law. It was there that he came in contact with the piety of the Pharisees and with the hope of Jews for the liberatin of the Holy Land, of the defeat and the vanquishing of the Romans by the sending of the Messiah, the Anointed One, who was to restore the glory of Israel and bring back to the Holy Land the Jews who had been dispersed throughout the world.

Within the Jewish community of Tarsus, Paul became aware of the discord existing between the Jews and the Gentiles. Paul was a man of high intelligence. Beyond his education he could form personal objective about the world. He was aware not only of the existing philosophies in Tarsus but also of the occult religions that people practiced there, coming from all over the world.

Paul's father was by profession a rich industrialist. He had a textile industry which specialized in the manufacture of a tough goat-hair fabric used in the making of tents. Young Paul obviously was apprenticed to the family business and he became a very skillful tentmaker. A principle rule in most Pharisee families. Even today it sounds modern: "It is good to study the Mosaic law, but in relation to a certain wordly profession, trade or occupation". Why was Paul apprenticed in such a hard manual occupation? It would not be of any use to him since he was studying to become rabbi.

The young intellectual could not imagine how valuable his skill in the craft of tentmaking would prove to be in the years to come. Learning a craft as hard as that of tentmaking would have meant hard work for the young Paul. It was just as hard as that of the carpenter. Here we should not forget that every evening when Paul finished his work in Tarsus at the family workshop, another boy in Nazareth would do the same, but the boy in Tarsus knew nothing of the boy in Nazareth.

On the basis of the Epistles of Paul, their form and content, we can draw certain conclusions regarding Paul's eduction. Paul possessed profound theological and legal learning. He was also very proficient in Greek. His proficiency was acquired not in Jerusalem but earlier in Tarsus. The Jews who had spread throughout the world were exposed to the infuence of the urban centres where they lived and worked. The Greek languaage, which was the nost appropriate and common instrument of communication, was taught, no doubt, in the schools of the Jewish communities of Tarsus as well.

One should recognise that Paul, by learning Greek, had also acquired further knowledge about the Hellenistic world. Paul proved himself to be a great orator. His belief in what he said and taught made his preaching attractive and convincing. He used the language like a master of philology. Paul gave the Greek language once more the vitality and the power that it had lost during the centuries. In spite of all this. Paul calls himself "unskilled in speaking" (cf. 2.Corinthians 11,6), because he did not acquire his eloquence in Greek by studying in a school of rhetoric or by reading rhetorial works.

According to an old tradition of the rabbis, a Jew at five years of age should start reading the "Tora" (the law), at ten he should study the "Mishna" (the oral tradition), at fifteen he should deal with the "Talmud" (the teachings) and at eighteen he should get married. When Paul reached the age of fifteen he had to move to Jerusalem to attend the famous University of the Temple. He was sent there to study and become a rabbi himself.

In modern terms, " dean of the College" in Paul's time was Gamaliel. According to St. Luke (cf. Acts 5,34), he was "a teacher of the law, held in honour by all the people". Gamaliel was the gratest Jewish teacher of the day, acknowledged by all as "Rabban", that is great master of the law.

Gamaliel had taken even the Apostles under his protection as we read in Acts 5,33 ff. It was the time when Peter and the other Apostles were arrested and were brought to the Supreme Court of the Jews. He asked that the court sit in camera and advised the members of the Sanhedrin not to take drastic measures against the Apostles. "So in the present case I tell you", said Gamaliel, "keep away from these men and let them alone; for if this plan or this undertaking is of men, it will fail; but if it is of God, you will not be able to overthrow them. You might even be found opposing God!".

Paul became a student of Gamaliel and acquired a profound biblical knowledge especially in using the triple interpretation of the meaning of the Bible. Life for Paul in Jerusalem was something new. He entered the high society of the Jewish polity, of the rulling establishment. The Jewish aristocratic society of Jerusalem spoke Aramaic with a fine pronunciation. They were polite and they were happy to invite people like Paul to their homes.

Their daughters, dressed according to the latest fashion and adorned with jewels, must have been attractive to young scholars who had come to study and who were obliged by Jewish tradition to get married at the age of eighteen. All these attractions were of no importance in relation to the religious zeal of young Paul. That is why he did not marry in spite of the fact that marriage was obligatory for the rabbis. His refusal to do so made a strong impression on Jewish society. However, there were other great leaders in Jewish history who remained unmarried too, like Elijah and Jeremiah.

Paul was only attracted by the Bible. He had commited most of it to memory in both languages, Hebrew and Greek. This memorizing of the Bible helped him a lot in later years. When he was travelling on foot on his missionary trips it was impossible for him to carry with him the voluminous and precious manuscripts of the Bible. In his thirteen Epistles one can count more than two hundred passages from the Old Testament.

Saul, the Persecutor of the Christians

We do not know if Paul met Jesus in person. Paul however gives a certain hint (cf. 2 Corinthians 5,16). Ten years had passed since Paul finished his studies in Jerusalem. Now in his late twenties (cf. Acts 7,58) he came back to Jerusalem. It is not known where he had been during the ten years that elapsed. He might have visited some Jewish communities abroad. He might have returned a few times to Jerusalem. However it is certain that his visits to the holy city had never been long, so that he had never had a chance to meet Jesus personally. If he had met Jesus, he would have mentioned it, especially, when his enemies questioned his apostolicity.

A man like Paul, with a furious character, could not have remained neutral. He had to choose between two directions, either to fight Jesus or to become his follower. Paul, being for the most of this time away from Jerusalem and not having met Jesus in person, remained indifferent. But now the time came for him to intervene in the critical affairs of Jerusalem Jewry. There were some Jews, mostly from Galilee and Jerusalem, who believed and declared in public that Jesus, who had been crucified, was the expected Messiah. This movement had attracted an alarming number of men and women. There were also people who believed that the movement would perish like that of Theudas and the other of Judas the Galilean (cf. Acts 5,36 ff). But this time things looked different.

The lion of Juda had roared and the whole world had heard it. Paul was one of those who had heard it from far away. For him the dead Jesus was more dangerous than the living one. The number of his followers was increasing constantly. Among them there was a famous Levite, Joseph the Cyprian, the friend and schoolmate of Paul, who himself had become a Nazarene and was now known under the name of Barnadas. Barnadas was so enthusiastic about the new religion that he sold a field that belonged to him and brought the money and laid it at the Apostles' feet (Acts 4,36-37).

The critical situation developing in Jerusalem made Paul travel there at once. His arrival there coincides with the persecution of Stephen. Stephen was one of the seven deacons apponted by the local church to take care of the Christians in need. He was of great ability and a fine orator. He was the first to understand the world importance of the Christian Church. Through his teaching he was obliged to attack the whole system of interpretation of the Bible (cf. Acts 6,8-15 and 7,1-60). The cardinal historic mistake of Judaism was that it blocked the whole perspective of human history by using the stone of the law and of the Temple. Furthermore Judaism wanted to stop the development of divine live for the human race. The result of this conflict was the stoning to death of Stephen.

Stephen was charged with blasphemy. The penalty was death by stoning. Here we should make a distinction. The Jewish religion court could only find a man worthy of punishment, in this case, of deat. It was the duty of the local Roman authority to issue the order for the execution. Pontius Pilate, the man who had held the office of procurator of Judea for so many years, was gone. The fanatic Jews could not wait for his successor. They decided to dispence with formality, to apply the lynch law and put Stephen to death their own way.

Lynching, however, had to be based on the Bible. According to Deuteronomy (17, 6-7) they needed three or at least two witnesses who would start the stoning. So they did. The first pushed Stephen down. The second took a heavy stone and threw it with all his power at the martyr. Then if he was still alive it was the turn of the pople to finish the job. The fanatical mob did so with great pleasure.

Paul was there, consenting to Stephen's death. It was in his care that the stoning-party left their cloaks, so that they could do the stoning unencumbered. In the Pinacotheca Vatican in Rome one can see the stoning of Stephen on one of the tapestries designed by Raphael for the Sistine Chapel. (This chapel is the principal one in the Vatican, famous for its frescoes by Michelangelo and other artists. It was built by order of pope Sixtus IV). Stoning was slow and protracted. The victim suffered unspeakably. It impressed Paul to see how courageously the martyr met his death, firm in his faith. " And as they were stoning Stephen, he prayed: Lord Jesus, receive my spirit. And he knelt down and cried with a loud voice: Lord do not hold this sin against them. And when he had said this, he fell asleep".

The criminal act had been brought to an end. This lynching of the martyr made people happy but not Paul. His conscience started bothering him. The tragic picture of Stephen's brutal death in the name of Mosaic law kept coming back to Paul's memory (cf. Acts 26,10; Galatians 1,23 and 1 Corinthians 15,9). "For I am the least of the apostles, unfit to be called an apostle, because I persecuted the church of God". Stephen's brutal death was the price that the early church had to pay in order to break Jewish nationalism and become a church of oecumenical dimensions. It was this oecumenical church that won to herself the great Apostle of the nations who carried out this historic separation.

There is no great victory without great cost. This is a basic principle even in the kingdom of God. Stephen offered this sacrifice and became the pioneer who led the way to a universal future. God may allow the individual to fail, but the mission continues. Stephen, the man of great ability and remarkable beauty, the deacon who worked wonders, the great hope of the early church, was dead. Truth, however, cannot vanish, cannot die, because God is behind it. Who could imagine at the time of Stephen's stoning, that within less than a year one of his killers, Paul, would take over Stephen's position and accomplish victoriously the cause for which Stephen offered his life! This is one of the miracles that Christianity works. It is the transformation of killers into saints.

Paul faced religion seriously and with absolute sincerity. Men like him cannot stand falsehood and hypocrisy for long, no matter how great the historic power these may possess. One may ask: What would Paul have been if there was no road to Damascus? Would he have become a teacher of Mosaic law or a leader of the movement for the liberation of the Holy Land? Would he have co-operated with Rome as Josephus Flavius (the Jewish historian and military leader) did later on or would he have become a sort of Greek style philosopher? There were many roads. His character would have pushed him to follow one of them.

There are many ways to the truth. There are a few people who by the grace of God find truth without difficulty at all. However there are others who have to fight an inner struggle, like Augustine (the latin church father; bishop of Hippo, in northern Africa; known for his "Confessions" and "The city of God") or Dante (the Italien poet who wrote "The Divine Comedy") did. Paul was led to the truth, passing first through a night of sin. He refers to two important things in his life; his hatred for the Christians and his experience on the road to Damascus. Paul accuses himself, but as he grows older, he thinks indulgently and says that he did what he did through ignorance. In spite of all this every single detail presses his mind and makes him experience a nightmare.

Stephen's brutal death marked the beginning of new persecutions of the new religion, it speeded up their momentum. Experience teaches us that the persecution of an innocent attracts people's sympathy. The very fact that Stephen died with a prayer of forgiveness on his bleeding lips made even Paul think about it. In spite of that, because Paul believed that he was right in persecuting the Christians, he started again. He had to finish his job no matter how hard it was.

He undertook the role of arresting the members of the new heresy and of bringing htem before the Jewish high court in Jerusalem, the Sanhedrin. There started a very close house - to house inquisition in which Paul took the lead. The followers of Christ fled as far as they cold go. Only the Apostles, the hard core of the innovators, remained in Jerusalem. It was early for the primitive church to go underground as it did later, in Rome and elsewhere. Paul did his job well in Jerusalem and wanted to expand abroad.

The method of persecuting the Christians was very clever indeed. The fanaticism of the Jewish masses was provoked through slander. This was done according to secret instructions issued by the Sanhedrin. Its members did not want the people to know that they were behind the persecutions. As soon as public opinion was roused against the Christians, Paul would appear and take over. It was a sort of Holy Inquisition. Paul was appointed the chief inquisitor. He had at his disposal everything that he needed: informers, the guardians of the Temple and full powers to arrest the Nazarenes, as many as possible. In Acts 26, 10-11 we read: *"And I did so in Jerusalem; I not only shut up many of the saints in prison, by authority from the chief priest, but when they were put to death I cast my vote against them. And I punished them often in all the synagogues and tried to make them blaspheme; and in raging fury against them, I persecuted them even to foreign cities."*

The purge was going on successfully. Arrests during the night. House-to-house inquisition. Oppressions, whippings and tortures would take place in the basements of each synagogue. Prisons became full. So the Nazarenes scattered. Those who could flee, would take their families and go away, even abroad, to the famous ancient city of Damascus.

News came that the new religion was gaining ground there. Paul's informers were everywhere. There was no place secure for those under persecution. *"But Saul laid waste the church, and entering house after house, he dragged off men and women and commited them to prison." (Acts 8,3)*. Paul was informed that the local authorities in Damascus were ready to co-operate with the Jewish hierarchy of Jerusalem, obviously for political reasons. *"But Saul, still breathing threats and murder against the dispiples of the Lord, went to the high priest and asked him for letters to the synagogues at Damaskus, so that if he found any belonging to the Way, men or women, he might bring them bound to Jerusalem" (Acts 9,1-2)*.

The *"expectation for the coming day"* was prevailing over the religious life of the Jews of Paul's time. There were also another two factors that dominated every activity of the Jews: the law and the last judgement. The law had 248 commandments and 346 prohibitions beyond the innumerable oral traditions. It was this frame of mind that one could wait for the day of the last judgement. This day had been depicted in the most dearing apocalyptic visions. He who would attempt to shake even the smallest stone of these foundatins of Judaism, had to be smashed. The whole set of commandments that had to do with morality or worship were of divine nature. The violation of one would mean the violation of all. The unbroken unity of the law was a dogma.

Paul was against any inefficient measures. He represented the order of the absolute. It is only in this way that his fanatism against Christians can be explained. According to this, everything was in perfect order with Paul's conscience. He fought the enemies of his faith. But there was something that bothered him. The way in which his enemies accepted persecutions and most of all death. The bearing of the martyrs' was the most effective argument in favour of the new religion. Death, even brutal, was observed by the martyrs with absolute constancy. One could see an inner relation of those departing this life with Jesus. They were absolutely sure that they were not entering the dark kingdom of death but the bright kingdom of enternal life. This was a light coming from another world. The Mosaic law could not be its source. It was impossible.

The martyrs' reactions confused Paul. He resisted any further thoughts, but the facts penetrated his inner world deeper and deeper with every day that passed. It was much late that Paul realized this deceptive power of "sin" and its demonic craft. Wrong religious education and up-bringing could be the cause of much unhappiness in life, could produce false peace and finally lead to lack of confidence in God. Paul the Christian, after Damascus, managed to be on good terms with his past and settle his inner life satisfactorily. He had not the sick feeling of an apostate. He did not deny his old values. He simply recognized their transient and temporary meaning. He faces his past in full tranquillity. His whole life should be understood as a unity, full of meaning for him and the mission he had to accomplish.

On the Way to Damascus:
Paul's Conversion

The appearance of Jesus to Paul was like a summer thunderbolt, for both Jews and Christians. Paul was called by Jesus, according to usual criteria, at the most unsuitable moment of his life; during the time of Paul's persecution of the church of Christ. The experience of Paul on the way to Damascus was, without doubt, one of the most dramatic in the history of man. It changed the history of the whole world. By the grace of God, the most savage persecutor of Christianity was transformed into the Apostle of the nations.

In this experience before the gate of Damascus the ex-Pharisee recognised the hand of God, who had intervened, all of a sudden and in a miraculous way, to reveal the Son of God, whom Paul was persecuting in the cruellest way. Paul felt his conversion and call as something unexpected and marvellous. Paul's conversion and call is described by St. Luke in the Acts of the Apostles in three places. By reading all three a full picture can be drawn, since each narration supports the other two (*).

The first basic account: Acts 9,1 - 19:

"But Saul, still breathing threats and murder against the disciples of the Lord, went to the high priest and asked him for letters to synagogues at Damascus, so that if he found any belonging to the Way, men or women, he might bring them bound to Jerusalem. Now as he journeyed he approached Damascus, and suddenly a light from heaven flashed about him. And he fell to the ground and heard a voice saying to him, "Saul, Saul, why do you persecute me?" And he said, "Who are

---

(*) *The English translation of the Greek original text is done, in comparison with existing translations, by the author himself, who is a specialist. This ensures purity of text. The Greek text used is that edited by Dr Everhard Nestle and revised by Dr. Erwin Nestle, sixteenth edition, as well as the text that is authorized by the Oecumenical Patriarchate of Constantinople.*

you, Lord?" And he said "I am Jesus, whom you are persecuting; but rise and enter the city, and you will be told what you are to do." The men who were travelling with him stood speechless, hearing the voice but seeing no one. Saul arose from the ground; and when his eyes were opened, he cold see nothing; so they led him by the hand and brought him into Damascus. And for three days he was without sight, and neither ate nor drank".

The second account: Acts 22,6-11:

"As I made my journey and drew near to Damascus, about noon a great light from heaven suddenly shone about me. And I fell to the ground and heard a voice saying to me, "Saul, Saul, why do you persecute me?" And I answered, "Who are you, Lord?" And he said to me, "I am Jesus of Nazareth whom you are persecuting." Now those who were with me saw the light but did not hear the voice of the one who was speaking to me. And I said "What shall I do, Lord?" And the Lord said to me, "Rise and go into Damascus, and there you will be told all that is appointed for you to do." And when I could not see because of the brightness of that light, I was led by the hand by those who were with me, and came into Damascus".

The third account: Acts 26,12-18:

"Thus I journeyed to Damascus with the authority and commission of the chief priests. At midday, O king!, I saw on the way a light from heaven, brighter than the sun, shining round me and those who journeyed with me. And when we had all fallen to the ground, I heard a voice saying to me in the Hebrew language, "Saul, Saul, why do you persecute me? It hurts you to kick against the goads." And I said, "Who are you, Lord?" And the Lord said "I am jesus whom you are persecuting. But rise and stand upon your feet; for I have appeared to you for this purpose, to appoint you to serve and bear witness to the things in which you have seen me and to those in which I will appear to you, delivering you from the people and from the Gentiles-to whom I send you to open their eyes, that they may turn from darkness to light and from the power of Satan to God, that they may receive forginess of sins and a place among those who are consecrated by faith in me."

Paul looking back at his life divides it into two main parts. The persiod "without Christ" and the period "in Christ". The

Damascus vision was the decisive turning point. Paul was like the hunter who had become obsessed by a mania for hunting. But he was not the only hunter. Somebody else, the Master of the disciples, followed his tracks. Paul thought that he chased, but he did not realize that he was being pursued. He had been travelling for eight days. The distance between Jerusalem and Damascus was about 250 kilometres if one followed the shortest way. He had in his pocket the letter of authority written by the high priest of Jerusalem.

He felt hate for the people who would destroy his faith. He knew that the victory of the Nazarenes would mean the end of the religion of the Jews and also the end of their plans for conquering the world. He felt that if the Nazarenes were right, even only on this point, the case was lost for ever. Everything he believed in, his whole world, stood or fell because of that. It was a question of his very spiritual existence, his life or his death. However he could not forsee that through this thought he was catching the truth. This was Paul's history-making inner condition. He would never become a Christian all by himself. At hearing the words *"Saul, Saul why do you persecute me?"* Paul felt an inner shock. He realized at once that the case was lost for him. Stephen was right. Jesus was alive. The question: *"Who are you Lord?"* does not betray any doubt but only surprise. Then follow the redeeming words, *"I am Jesus whom you are persecuting"*. Through this event faith in Jesus had dawned in Paul's life.

It was the full conclusion of a treaty signed by Paul's mind and will, which had revolted against God. It was a captivity of all Paul's thoughts. In his heart there was no doubt about what he had experienced during these few moments. Paul was convinced that he had really seen, met and talked with the risen Christ. When Paul arose from the ground, he was already a faithful follower of Jesus feeling absolutely the call to become the Apostle of the nations.

Every genuine conversion is marked by two stages: the return of the mind and the return of the heart. Psychology of Religion cannot explain basically how the inner transformation and the building of the new religious inner world of Paul was done. Paul needed three days to remove the ruins of his old philosophy and way of life. We should emphasize here that Paul was neither a shipwreck nor a weak character as some want to portray him to-day. He was proud and stiff. He had been struck on his way but he would not be subjugated to anybody else except Jesus.

Paul was a very sincere man. The Sunday following his conversion and call he felt the need to explain to the members of the synagogue what had happened to him, that is, the change in his thought, his mid and his actions. He made his explanations by simply proclaiming Jesus. Here is how Luke describes it in Acts 9, 19-25: *"For several days he was with the disciples at Damascus. And in the synagogues immediately he proclaimed Jesus, saying, "He is the·Son of God." And all who heard him were amazed, and said, "Is not this the man who made havoc in Jerusalem of those who called on this name? And he has come here for this purpose, to bring them bound before the chief priests". But Saul increased all the more in strength, and confounded the Jews who lived in Damascus by proving that Jesus was the Christ. When many days had passed, the Jews plotted to kill him, but their plot became known to Saul. They were watching the gates day and night, to kill him; but his disciples took him by night and let him down over the wall, lowering him in a basket."*

This was Paul's first flight. He had to run away. From now on his life would be a continuous history of brave flight like the life of his Master.

Paul's Personality

Paul's conversion and Paul's call to become the Apostle of the nations were one and the same thing. The voice that he heard on the Damascus road was for him an order that he go to nations and proclaim Him who had been revealed to him. Paul, however, was not the first who had undertaken to preach the gospel to the Gentiles. There were other people before him who had prepared the way, but he was the one who would establish and organize the local churches in the oecumene, in the world. He was the first after the One, the great Apostle of the nations, who suffered and toiled more than any other of the Apostles.

Paul belonged to that category of people, who are moved to action by their inner experiences and who utilize their soul to the utmost for that which they are after. As a Pharisee he was possessed by such a zeal that nothing could stop him from doing what he considered right. Now that he was an Apostle, nothing could stop him from doing what he considered right. Now that he was an Apostle, nothing could stop him performing his duty and carrying out his perilous mission. He had to face dangers on land and on the high seas, the mania of Jews against him, the intrigues of the pseudo-brothers, and even the illness of his own body. Paul had been afflicted with "a thorn in the flesh", a mysterious disease, which he does not specify but which scholars suspect to be "malaria", contracted originally in the marshes of Tarsus. (Malaria is characterized by severe chills and fever. It is an infectious disease, generally intermittent and recurrent. It is transmitted to man by the bite of an infected anopheles mosquito). Paul's ceaseless fight is a basic element of his character, of his natural disposition, of his very existence.

Paul was also distinguished by his conviction that he was the emissary of God and that he had to accomplish his great mission. His certainly about the grandeur of the work that God had assigned to him constituted a vital source of strengh for him and was one of the basic reasons for his success. The deep love that Paul felt for Christ constituted another reason for his success. But Paul loved the people also. It is this multi-faceted love and affection which explains his devotion; he did not retreat in the face of danger or sacrifice. The most touching sacrifice that Paul's love imposed on himself is that during all these years of travelling he worked as a tentmaker in order to make a living, in order to provide his fellows too with the necessaries of life. He did it, no matter how hard it was, simply because he wanted to keep his gospel free of any charge.

Paul's adaptability is also something that one has to admire in him. He was helped greatly by his capacity to understand the psychlogical problems of the people. Paul was a great diplomat. He could handle people and difficult situations excellently and with truth. Here we should emphasize however that in questions of faith Paul could not compromise. He was firm in what he believed in and what he proclaimed as "the truth".

Paul, although an optimist, was not a romantic utopian for whom reality did not exist. He was continually aware of differing situations. He knew how to exploit and utlize with prudence for the benefit of his gospel. Above all Paul knew how to handle and direct people and disturbed souls. His Epistles testify to the fact that he would not turn away by the fullness of his heart, but that he thought, wrote and acted through a deep knowledge of the people and a meticulous study of the circumstances. His burning enthusiasm for his mission and his call, and his devoted and sacrificial love did not prevent him from being able to look at the realities of life with a crystal clear eye and each time utilise the means that would best serve his mission to the world.

PART TWO

The Apostle of the Nations
His Journeys in Brief

Through his experience on the road to Damascus Paul became a new man, he acquired a new personality, almost a new "ego", which was moving now by the grace of God towards new goals. Paul's vision is one of the most dramatic in history since, it has changed the world itself. Many in the world of art throughout the centuries have attempted to visualise the even in colour or in poetry. Painters and hymnologists portrayed, each one in his own way, the mysterious phenomenon, the miracle, that won for Paul the freedom which God had reserved for him from his mother's womb.

In Damascus Paul was baptized by Ananias. His baptism marks the crossing over a line from death to life, which the great Apostle had already passed as "a chosen vessel" of the grace of God. In the big city Paul proclaimed Jesus, after having been a notorious persecutor of the faithful and a devoted Pharisee.

In the letter to the Galatians (1,17) we read that Paul after his conversion "went away into Arabia" and that he "returned to Damascus". We do not know the reason for this journey to Arabia. In the Acts there is no mention of such a trip. This is a period of Paul's life that needs illumination.

By Arabia here is meant the kingdom of the Nabateans, whose capital was the rock-hewn, inaccessible city of Petra. Upon his return to Damascus the local Jews reacted to his teaching there. They organized a conspiracy to liquidate him, but their plot became known to Paul. They were watching the gates day and night to kill him; but his disciples sent him away by night. In this way Paul escaped and went to Jerusalem, just three years after his conversion and call.

At that time, Aretas IV was the king of the land (2

Corinthians 11, 32-33). He became its possessor in the years of Caligula (AD 37-41) and after the death of Tiberius (AD37). King Aretas lived up to AD 40, consequently Paul's conversion took place in AD 35 or 36.This is in full agreement with the information given to us in the letter to the Galatians (2,1), according to which Paul went to Jerusalem for the second time after fourteen years, that is after the vision on the road to Damascus. It was during his second visit to Jerusalem that the Apostolic Synod took place (AD 49).

During his first visit there he stayed *"with Cephas only fifteen days. He saw none of the other apostles except James, the Lord's brother"* (cf. Galatians 1,18-19). But the Jews had not forgotten him. In Acts 22,17-21 we read: *"When I had returned to Jerusalem and was praying in the temple, I fell into a trance and saw him saying to me, "Make haste and get quickly out of Jerusalem, because they will not accept you testimony about me". And I said, "Lord, they themselves know that in every synagogue I imprisoned and beat those who believed in thee. And when the blood of Stephen thy witness was shed, I also was standing by and approving, and keeping the garments of those who killed him". And he said to me, "Depart"; for I will send you far away to the Gentiles".*

So Paul returned to his home city, Tarsus. There he was visited by Barnabas and together they went to Antioch. It was in Antioch that the Nazarenes were named for the first time in history "Christians" "χριστιανοί", that is Men of Christ. That meant the creation of a third race alongside Jews and Greeks. During those days there was a great famine and the Cristians in Antioch *"determined, every one according to his ability, to send relief to brethren who lived in Judea; and they did so, sending it to the elders by the hand of Barnabas and Paul"* (Acts 11,28-30). They, having fulfilled their mission there, returned to Antioch *"bringing with them John whose other name was Mark"* (Acts 12,25), that is the nephew of Barnabas.

Antioch was the base of operations for Paul. The history of Paul's missionary journeys, the reverse campaign of Alexander the Great, from Eat to the West, started there, from that great and famous city.

A brief account of Paul's itineraries follows here, but without any comments. It is in the third part of this book, under the title "Paul and Hellas Unbound", that Paul's journeys to Cyprus and Greece are dealt with in detail and where all known information is given with comments.

The First Missionary Journey in Brief
(cf. Acts chapters 13 and 14)

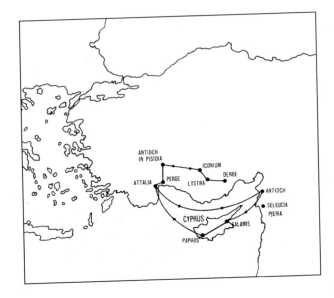

The journey included Cyprys, Attalia, Perge, Antioch in Pisidia, Iconium and Derbe. It seems that this journey had as its main object the large communities of Jews in Cyprus. It was Barnabas who led the way and had the command. The method of the Apostles was to start proclaiming Jesus first to the Jews in the synagogues. The reaction of the Jews was hostile. The Apostles had to turn to the Gentiles mostly through the Hellenized Jews.

It is astonishing to notice that in the places visited during the first missionary journey the establishing of christian communities according to the model of the church in Antioch (where the majority was jewish) was not possible. The small nucleus of churches established in Cyprus and in Asia Minor had mostly as its members converted Gentiles. Looking at the first from this side we find it very successfull (cf. Acts 14,23), though it was done at the expense of many dangers, persecutions, and hardships.

The Second Missionary Journey in Brief

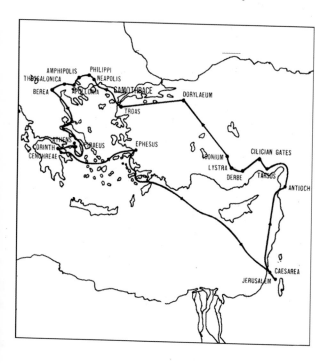

Paul, escorted by Silas, travelled by land starting from Antioch. They passed Tarsus, the Cilician Gates, Derbe and reached Lystra where Timothy joined them. They went on to Dorylaeum, and stopped at Troas. There a man of Macedonia appeared to Paul in a vision telling him "Come over to Macedonia and help us" (Acts 16,10). They sailed to Samothrace and landed at Neapolis. In Philippi they ended up in jail, charged with anti-Roman activities. They were freed in a miraculous way and then, through Amphipolis and Apollonia, they reached Thessalonica and Veria. Paul alone reached Athens and finally Corinth, having travelled by sea. In Corinth Paul stayed for one and half years. Then, escorted by Aquila and Priscilla, came to Ephesus. From there he travelled to Caesaria of Palestine, remained a short time in Jerusalem and came back to his base, Antioch.

40

The Third Missionary Journey in Brief

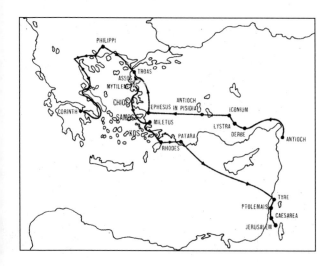

Paul starting from Antioch and travelling through South Galatia and Phrygia, came back to Ephesus as he had promised (Acts 18,21 "I will return to you if God wills"). Ephesus became a base of operations for the next three years. It is from here that Paul visited Asia Minor, Greece and other places. Luke, the physician, the author of the Acts, gives us a very incomplete picture of Paul's missionary activities during this period. Much is not mentioned. Nothing is said for example about a short trip to Corinth where he was ill-treated and was obliged to retun immediately to Ephesus. Also nothing is mentioned about a mission to Illyricum (cf. Epistle to the Romans 15,19) that must have taken place during this period.

Paul, having left Ephesus and Asia Minor after the uprising of the mob, travelled through Macedonia and arrived in Corinth where he remained for htree months. He had intended to return to Syria by sea but he changed his mind and returned by land through Macedonia, prolonging his stay in Philippi, where he

Athens: St. Dionysius the Areopagite, the first bishop of Athens, venerated as the patron saint of the city of Athens. Mosaic in the homonum church on Skoufa Street, Kolonaki.

Cyprus Salamis: The Ancient Theatre.

met Luke. From Philippi they sailed to Troas. The voyage took them five days. Having stayed in Troas for almost a week, Paul walked to Assos and from there they sailed to Mytilene, Samos and Chios and landed at Miletus. From Miletus they continued their voyage through Cos and Rhodes to Patara and farther to Tyre, Ptolemais, Caesarea, finally reaching Jerusalem.

In Jerusalem he escaped death and was sent as prisoner to the Governor Felix in Caesarea being escorted by a detachment of two hundred infantry and seventy horsemen under the leadership of two Roman centurions. Paul's captivity in Caesarea lasted two years (AD 57-59?). At that time Felix was called to Rome. Porcius Festus came to Judaea as procurator. During Festus' visit to Jerusalem, the leaders of the Jews asked him to send Paul back to Jerusalem. Their plan was to murder Paul on the way. Paul, realizing that a trial in Caesarea presided at by Festus would mean death for him and that he would undoubtedly be sacrificed to political expediency, appealed to Caesar, as he was entitled to do, being a Roman citizen.

The Fourth Missionary Journey in Brief

Paul had appealed to Caesar. The imperial court that tried him, found him innocent and released him. According to the information that we receive from the letter to the Corinthians of Clement, Bishop of Rome, Paul, after his release from his Roman captivity, travelled to Spain. The same journey took him to the East too, that is to Asia Minor, Crete, Macedonia and the territory of Illyricum-Dalmatia. According to Paul's Second Letter to Timothy he returned to Rome, where he was arrested and about to be executed. It was then that Paul wrote this letter, to Timothy, Paul's "swan song", telling him to "do his best and go to him" (cf 2 Timothy 4,9). "For I am already", Paul writes, "on the point of being sacrificed; the time of my departure has come. I have fought the good fight, I have finished the race, I have kept the faith. Henceforth there is laid up for me the crown of righteousness, which the Lord, the righteous judge, will award to me on that Day, and not ony to me but also to all who have loved his appearing". (2 Timothy 4,6-8).

According to old church tradition Paul stood a second trial in Rome and perished in the Neronian persecution of AD 67. However, for the sake of scientific accuracy we should notice that the period between Paul's first and second captivities in Rome is covered by a thick mist through which modern science tries to see and find facts which are beyond doubt. However, it is certain that Paul was beheaded outside the walls of Rome.

His life, full of sacrifice and activity, started in the Hellenistic city of Tarsus and ended in the eternal city of Rome.

Suggested Chronology

The chronology of the life and journeys of Paul is not with accuracy fixed. We take as the basis the time when Porcius Festus came to Caesarea (Judaea) as procurator in succession to Felix who was recalled to Rome. This event marks the end of the two-year captivity of Paul in Caesarea. But we do not know exactly when this change occured.

We can also calculate Paul's cloudy chronology on the basis of an inscription found at Delphi and published by the Frenchman Emil Bourguet (cf. De rebus Delphicis 1905, p. 63). On this inscription it is mentioned that Claudius after a military victory was proclaimed for the 26th time emperor (a typical honourary distinction that had nothing to do with the thirteen years of his reign). On the inscription it is further mentioned that this event happened when the proconsul of Achaia (Corinth being its capital) was Lucius Junius Gallio, a brother of Seneca, the philosopher. This Galio is mentioned in Acts 17,12, *"But when Galio was proconsul of Achaia, the Jews made a united attack upon Paul and brought him before the tribunal.."*. It was during Paul's first visit to Corinth and the establishing of the christian community there. Through the fixing of the chronology of the event mentioned on the inscription of Delphi, that is, of the time of the 26th proclamation of Claudius as emperor, we can fix also the chronology of Paul.

One also should bear in mind that the presence of Aquila and Priscilla in Corinth gives us a date before which Paul could not have been in Corinth. Claudius had ordered the expulsion of the Jews from Rome and Italy in AD 49. It was then that Aquila and Priscilla had travelled to Corinth and were met by Paul there.

Science, however, cannot fix two things. First, the time of the 26th proclamation of Claudius, and second, the duration of Gallio's stay as proconsul in Corinth-Achaia.

On the basis that during Stephen's stoning and death (AD 33 or 34) Paul was a young man ("νεανίας"), being at the same time a personality who was well known to the people in Jerusalem, we can calculate that he was then at least 25 years old. Consequently, he must have been born between AD 1 and 5. To this one should add that thirty years after the death of Stephen, Paul refers to himself as an old man ("presbytis") (cf. Philemon 9). This might imply that he was at least sixty years

---

Delphi: Delphi, the great cultural and athletic centre, the national conscience of the entire Greek world, was held in deep reverence by the Greeks. It was here that Emil Bourguet found the inscription which is connected with St. Pauls chronology (see text).

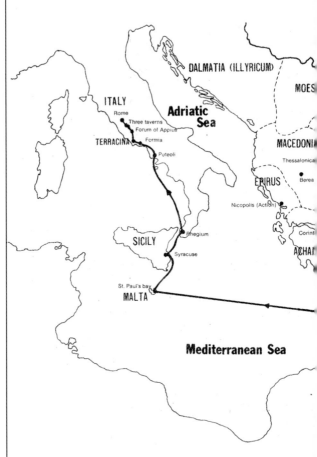

We obtain details about this journey from the Acts, chapters 27 and 28. Paul lived in Rome "two whole years at his own hired dwelling and welcomed all who came to him, preaching the kingdom of God and teaching about the Lord Jesus quite openly and unhindered" (cf. Acts 28,30-31).

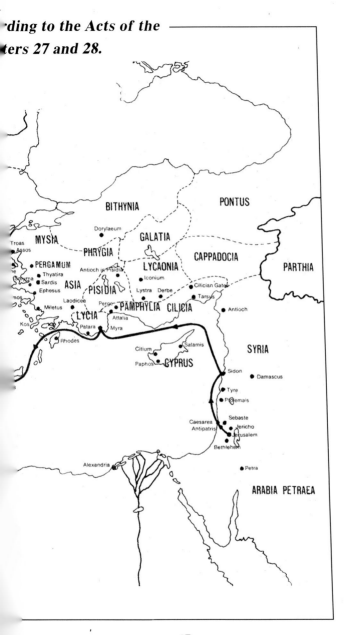

47

old. But in spite of all these indirect pieces of evidence, Paul's chronology remains imprecise.

Here is given a suggested chronology which is accepted by most scholars. One should notice, however, that it allows a difference of one to five or more years.

		The imperial throne of Rome was occupied by:
AD 1-5	Paul was born	
30	Christ was crucified	Augustus AD 14
33/34	(?) The stoning of Stephen	
	Conversion and Call of Paul	Tiberius AD 14-37
34-36	Paul's travel to Arabia	
36/37	First trip to Jerusalem	Caligula AD 37-41
37-42	Stay in Tarsus	
42	Arrival in Antioch	Claudius AD 41-54
44	Another trip to Jerusalem.	
45-48	First Missionary Journey	
49-52	Second Missionary Journey	
49/50	Neapolis-Philippi	
50/51	Thessaloniki-Veria	
51/52	Athens and Corinth	
	The writing of the First and Second	
	Epistles to the Thessalonians	
53-58	Third Missionary Journey	
54-57	Ephesus	Nero AD 54-68
54/55	The writing of the Epistle	
	to the Galatians	
56	The writing of the First Epistle	
	to the Corinthians	
57	Escape from Ephesus	
	The writing of the Second Epistle	
	to the Corinthians	
	Short journey to Illyricum	
57/58	Winter in Corinth	
	The writing of the Epistle	
	to the Romans	
58	Paul's last trip to Jerusalem	

58-60	Imprisonment in Caesarea
60/61	Journey to Rome according to the Acts, chapters 27 and 28
61-63	First captivity in Rome
	The writing of the Epistles of captivity
63-66	Journey to the East. Missionary journey to Crete, Spain etc.
66/67	Return from Spain
	Winter in Nicopolis-Actium
	The writing of the First Epistle to Timothy and of that to Titus
67	Second imprisonment in Rome
	The writing of the Second Epistle to Timothy
	MARTYRDOM IN ROME

Principles and Methods of Paul's Missionary Activities

Paul, in proclaiming God all over the world, followed certain principles and methods.

Principally, he avoided preaching in cities and territories where the new religion was known through the activities of other people. He chose mostly cities where there was a synagogue or cities that constituted commercial centres so that through the coming and going of the people they could easily widen the spread of the new ideas.

He hurried from one country to the next visiting the principal cities, being convinced that the day of the second coming of the Lord was near and therefore as many people as possible should get the chance to hear the message of God before He appeared again on earth. Teaching in the main cities was important for him. It was from these centres that the news would travel to the country.

The people who would carry the new ideas were of all

professions, crafts and trades. Merchants, slaves, free people, soldiers, all would bring the message to the nearby villages. The Jewish couple of Aquila and Priscilla, established in Rome, were already Christians when they were driven away from Italy to Corinth by the decree of the Roman Emperor Claudius concerning the explusion of the Jews from Rome. This is evidence that the christian community in Rome was founded before Paul or Peter had the chance to preach there.

Paul would start his teaching from the Synagogue not because Jews were the beloved people of God and therefore they had a priority in salvation, but mainly because it was there, in the Synagogue that he could establish contact with the Gentiles through their friends converted to Judaism. Usually Paul's teaching in the Synagogue would end up in a conflict with the Jews. It was then that he would turn directly to the Gentiles.

From the samples of his preaching that one may read in the Acts of the Apostles and in Paul's Epistles the multiple talents of the great man can be seen, his genius and his power of adaptability to differing situations. The form and the content of his teaching changes according to his audience. He approached Jews, Gentiles, or educated people in different ways.

Paul's teaching would naturally give ground for questions or misunderstandings. The local churches would question him, or he would learn about their problems from his associates. Paul's letters are full of his answers to their questions and problems. It was through letters and special emissaries that Paul would keep contact with his churches.

Those attracted by the message of Paul would enter the local church through "the baptism", the ritual through which they would get into a mysterious direct contact with God, the head of the Church. Then followed the "holy eucharist" and the worshipping of God in common prayer that would unite the members of the Church with the bonds of love.

Reactions to Paul's Activities

Paul's missionary work was hindered in many ways by many factors. Nothing he did was without reaction.

The first to react were the Gentiles who had been converted to Judaism. They were amongst those who tried each time to question Paul's apostolicity. This is why, in all hil letters, Paul, begins by emphasizing that he was an Apostle. The same group of people would spread rumours about the money that the people collected and sent to the other churches for the needs of their poor members. For this reason Paul would carry the moeny, mostly to Jerusalem, never alone but in common with a committee of people appointed by the local church. The same group of people would accuse Paul of misinterpreting the word of God. They would even refer to Paul's sufferings from malaria as a proof of God's disapproval of Paul's teaching.

Another group of people which reacted in a fierce and violent way against Paul's teaching were the Jews. They hated Paul for being an apostate and furthermore for being the one who interrupted their traditional work of converting Gentiles to Judaism. It was this that made them plot against Paul's life, made them accuse him as an enemy of the Roman state, and instigate the mob against Paul.

The third category of Paul's enemies was some of the Christians themselves.

Paul's enthusiasm for the new religion and his devotion to the duties ofthe Apostle of the nations would not be diminished by the multiple reaction against him and his work. There was nothing that would shake his strong belief in the victorious end of his attempts. The gospel of freedom had been proclaimed. Christianity had broken the ties that had kept it tied to Judaism as one entity. Thus Christianity elevated itself and became a universal religion as God had revealed it and as it was rightly understood by the great Apostle.

Paul's Writings

It has been said, and it is not an exaggeration, that it was not Paul the Apostle, but Paul the writer and author who won the victory over the world and laid and laid on its ruins the foundation of "the new heavens and the new earth", which he had undertaken to proclaim. Paul, in caring about the future of his churches, wrote to them letters, known as Epistles. They are letters to individuals, to local christian communities of the early church, to groups of such communities, or they are letters addressed to all; - circular letters. From all these letters thirteen only were accepted by the early church as genuine and were included in the New Testament.

Letter writing is an old way of communication. We have letters from classical antiquity written on marble, clay, stones etc. Paul's letters sometimes present a rhetorical form and the language used is rather formal and oratorical. This is because the author of the letters, did not write them by himself but dictated them, as was customary. Paul's Epistles constitute the best source for his life, theology, personality, character and way of thinking and acting.

The Results of Paul's Missionary Work

In evaluating Paul's work it is evident that through his devotion to his mission assigned to him by God, he succeeded in the following:

He established awareness of Christianity as a new religion. He separated it from Judaism and from the religions of the Greek world. Furthemore, he avoided the danger of Christianity falling into the form of a "legal religion", as was Judaism.

Paul's spirit has been alive in the universal church through the centuries. We all feel his presence in the institution whose survival he helped greatly, even by his martyrdom.

Paul, the Apostle of the nations, has been great indeed and remains great. Humanity should turn to him whenever it faces the risk of losing its real nature, whenever it wants to be reborn.

PART THREE

PAUL AND HELLAS UNBOUND
PAUL IN CYPRUS

Cyprus is one of the most beautiful islands of the Mediterranean Sea. It is an independent state, a republic. Eighty one per cent of its inhabitants are Greeks, eighteen per cent are of Turkish origin and the other one per cent is constituted of foreigners. The name of Cyprus is met for the first time in Homer's "Iliad" and "Odessey". In the "Iliad", we find the name "Cypris" as a surname of Venus. There are inscriptions that bear the name Cyprus dated 459 BC.

Contemporary historical nad archeological studies prove that the first inhabitants of the island were not the Phoenicians but the Greeks. The civilization created by them has not yet been fully investigated and studied, but it was as highly developed as that of the Minoan civilization in Crete. Inscriptions have been found dated earlier than the time when the Phoenicians predominated the island. They are Greek inscriptions expressed in a special kind of syllabic writing. Cyprus has a genuine Greek history of four thousand years.

Paul and Barnabas, escorted by Mark, the nephew of the latter, walked down to the harbour towns of Antioch, Seleucia and Pieria, and with the blessing of the local church started a new page, perhaps the most significant, in the history of civilization. Even today, on a clear day, one can see the old sunken pier at Seleucia. One of the two old breakwaters under the surface of the sea bears the name of Paul and the other of Barnabas.

Barnabas was an ex-hellenistic Jew from Cyprus and one of the first Christians. It was he who introduced Paul to he Apostles in Jerusalem and who went with Paul on his first journey.

In the course of history, many campaigns started from the harbour of Seleucia both before Paul's time and later on.

53

Mighty kings, famous generals and powerful armies of crusades. History has forgotten all of them. Their tracks have been erased by the wind of time. No trace of them can be seen there. The work that the three poor missionaries set out to do, that is, to preach Christ to the world, not only has remained alive, but has shaped history and the destiny of many peoples and nations. Paul's missionary journeys have been called a "Christian Odyssey". Not since the time of Homer had any ship set sail on a more courageous voyage. We do not know the name of that small Cyprian ship. Yet, unknown as it is, it is not of less importance than the flagship of Christopher Colombus, "The Santa Maria".

Barnabas suggested that they stop at Salamis, near modern Famagusta. To-day, the memory of Barnabas is greatly honoured there. According to an old church tradition, Barnabas was martyred there in AD 61. If Paul had been in command of this missionary journey it would have taken antother course. Paul was aware looking beyond sentimental lies, that Cyprus was not the crossroads of the transport and travel communications of the Roman empire. Paul could see clearly that he had to preach in the big centres if he expected the new religion to spread out quickly. Since Barnabas was the leader of the group, Paul complied with his suggestion to travel through Cyprus.

Old Salamis stood on the golden strand that still delights all visitors. The small ship carrying the three Apostles landed there. Salamis was at that time the biggest and most important harbour in Cyprus. To-day one can see the extensive ruins near Famagusta. The old ruined city dated back to before the invasion of the Phoenicians. Salamis is directly connected with the Trojan war. Its founder and first king was Teuctros the Telamonian, one of the most interesting persons in the history of the Trojan war. The district of modern Salamis-Famagusta is the richest in Cyprus for archeological treasures, which date from nearly four thousand years ago. At the Bronze Age site of Enkomi-Alasia we can see a bronze smelting house of the fourteenth century B.C. at famous Salamis, grand marble columns representing the flowering of Greek and Roman civilization; at medieval Famagusta the purest French style of Gothic architecture mingling with the simple Byzantine, and the finest military architecture of Venice and Genoa; in the far north the Lusignan mountain castle of Kantara and, out along the remote Karpas peninsula, some gems of Byzantine churches.

The ruins that we can see to-day along the beautiful, secluded, sandy beaches remind us of the bright and glorious city where the Greek civilization prevailed with a touch of Phoenician colour and a lively Jewish community. These Jews revolted during the reign of Marcus Ulpius Trajanus (AD 116-117), but their revolution was suppressed in the cruellest way and the flourishing city was devastated. This devastation by sword and fire was following by terrible earthquakes, which took place between AD 332 and 342. Salamis was rebuilt by a Christian emperor under the new name of Constantia, but it was again ruined during the seventh century by the Saracens and its inhabitants moved to the nearby city of Arsinoi, the modern Famagusta. The ruins of Salamis near the modern village of Ayios Seryios are varied: private buildings and public monuments, of which the most important are the magnificent market of the city and the bronze smelting houses. The ruins that were brought to light through various excavations belong to the historic times. The picture is being completed by the recently discovered prehistoric necropolis of Salamis.

Famagusta is five kilometres south of Salamis. It is located exactly where the king of Egypt, Ptolemy Philadelphus (285-247 BC) built the city which he named Arsinoi, in honour of his sister. During the Byzantine period the city was named Justiniani in honour of the emperor Justinian (AD 567-565), who created magnificent buildings there; his wife Theodora had been born in the city. Later the city was called by its modern Greek name Ammochostos, because of the golden strand that is to be found on the beautiful sandy beaches of the area.

Famagusta was a fabulously wealthy town in the Middle Ages, immortalized by Shakespeare in his Othello. The city is one of the most precious ensembles of medieval architecture in the world. We should notice, however, that Famagusta was nothing but a small fishing village up till the end of the thirteenth century. When the last crusade ended with the fall of Acre to the Arabs in 1291, many of the richest Christian merchants fled from the Holy Land to Cyprus and settled in Famagusta. Continuing their trade with the mainland, these merchants rapidly developed Famagusta into the richest town in the Mediterranean. There they are said to have built 365 churches as weel as the fine Gothic Cathedral of St. Nicholas and palatial private residences. The main square of the town was reputed to be the largest in Europe. To-day we can see this famous Cathedral, and the castle, but only a few of the churches.

It was in Salamis that Paul, Barnabas and Mark spent a few weeks, perhaps till they had spoken to the numerous synagogues of the area. Here the Jews of the diaspora were tolerant and there was no violent reaction.

Paul and his associates, having finished their mission in Salamis, started walking into the mountainous uplands, on the road along the river Pedieos which makes the area fertile. It was there that Herod the Great had brought many Jews and made them work in the bronze mines that Augustus had rented to him.

Cyprus is one hundred and fifty kilometres long from east to west Pliny informs us that there were in Cyprus fifteen main centres of habitation. If we suppose that the Apostles visited all of them and if they preached only once at each one of them, then it would have taken them at least fifteen weeks to cross the island. Small groups of Christians were formed in each one of these towns. They were to be better organized and directed later on by Barnabas.

The Apostles followed the old Roman road that led to Paphos, crossing first the area of Limassol. The modern city of Limassol is the nearest one to Egypt and the most important import and export harbour of the island. Limassol, the second largest town in Cyprus, is the heir of two great kingdoms of antiquity which are found on either side, on the sunny southern coast; Curium to the west and Amathus to the east. Limassol to-day is the busiest and most festive of the island's towns. It houses the bulk of the island's industries, including the major part of the great wine industry. Limassol became a famous town in the Middle Ages and it was here that Richard Coeur de Lion of England married Berengaria of Navarre and that the Knights Templar and the Knights of St. John of Jerusalem established their headquarters after the Arabs overan the Holy Land in 1291.

Cyprus Salamis: The Gymnasium.

Paul and his associates had to pass along the mountainous road and through the beautiful valleys that extend up into the Troodos hill, lined with tall silver-stemmed poplar trees and extensive cherry and apple orchards. To-day there are several popular resorts here. Mount Olympus- Troodos rises up over 2140 m above sea level and is carpeted with snow from January to March. The Troodos resorts and villages are rich in monuments of the long years of Byzantine rule in Cyprus; fine monasteries and little churches, often with exquisite interior wall-paintings. Elsewhere in the district there is also an abudance of interesting places, such as the celebrated Kolosso Castle, former headquarters of the Knights of St. John of Jerusalem and the Greco-Roman site at Curium, where we may see the remains of the famous Temple of Apollo, a theatre and some fine mosaic floors. The theatre has been restored in recent years and has become the setting for an annual festival of Greek and Shakespearean drama.

From Curium, Paul headed for Paphos, the city that seems to be the most ancient on the island. It is the birthplace of

Aphrodite the Cyprian (the foamborn), so named because she was supposed to have sprung from the sea (aphros- foam in Greek). Aphrodite in Greek mythology was the goddess of love and beauty, identified as Venus by the Romans.

In Greek theogony, that is the origin or genealogy of the gods as told in myths, as it has been delivered to us by Hesiod, it is mentioned that when Cronos had mutilated his father Uranus, he threw the remains of him into the sea. The sea formed then a superwhite foam through which Aphrodite the Anadyomene, (the emerging), the beautiful virgin was born and rose naked. Through the centuries, famous men of art, painters and sculptors, have tried to portray her, each one in his own way and imagination, as she emerged from the waves and the foam in all her brightness and magic splendour. Aphrodite, riding on a scallop shell, stepped ashore first on the island of Cythera; but finding this only a small island, passed on to the Peloponese. The picture of the birth of Aphrodite is completed by the "humn" to her that has its origin in Homer. It is in htis hymn that we learn that Zephyrus, (i.e. the personification of the west wind, considered by the Greeks to be the most mild and gentle of the sylvan deities), had moved her gently to the coast of Cyprus, the principal seat of her worship. As soon as the goddess of beauty and love touched the Cyprian land, anemones and other wild flowers appeared to surround the goddess in the most beautiful array of colours. Flowers continued to spring from the soil wherever she trod. They were the same kind of wild flowers that we see to-day among the broken marbles of the ancient temples of Paphos.

The Homerian hymn goes on to tell us that Aphrodite was welcomed in the Cyprian land with enthusiasm by the Seasons, the "Horai", the daughters of Zeus, who, wearing their golden diadems on their charmingly combed heads, had come to attend, to clothe and to adorn her with precious golden necklaces. They put a golden wreath on her head and escorted the young goddess to dwell on Mount Olympus (perhaps originally to the Cyprian one and later to that of Greece), among the other Olympian deities of Greek mythology.

We should notice here that Aphrodite is the same wide-ruling goddess who rose from Chaos and danced on the sea. We will find her later on in Corinth with her thousand courtesans on the Acrocorinth. In Syria and Palestine, Aphrodite was worshiped as Istar or Ashtaroh. To-day in Paphos her original aniconic image is still shown in the ruins of a grandiose Roman Aphrodite Temple. Aphrodite is accompanied by doves and sparrows, who were noted for their lechery in antiquity. Since life in the Greek theogony began in the sea, people in the Mediterranean countries regard sea food as an aphrodisiac. The Corinthians and the visitors of the city would pay their tribute to her on the Acrocorinth.

Modern Paphos offers a superb combination of beautiful scenery and places of historic and legendary interest. Ancient Greeks, Romans and the Byzantine and medieval rulers of Cyprus all left their mark on this part of the island. The modern capital of Paphos district is known as Ktima. It is a beautifully laid-out little town, superbly situated on a rocky escarpment overlooking the sea and the historic harbour of New Paphos. Ktima is the successor to New Paphos, the capital of Cyprus during Roman times. New Paphos today is a tiny picturesque harbour, which in Roman times was one of the grandest harbours of the Empire, and traces of the old works may still be seen. Among the famous Roman governors of Cyprus who resided at New Paphos were the orator Cicero and Sergius Paulus, the first governor in the Empire to be converted to Christianity. In New Paphos we may see, in the grounds of Chrysopolitissa Church, a pillar to which Paul is said to have been bound and scourged during his visit to New Paphos. The whole area of New Paphos is rich in historic remains, from the castle and ancient wall defences to the fascinating Tombs of the Kings. These tombs, of which tere are about one hundred, are carved out of the solid rock underground, some containing Doric pillars, of royal magnificence, hence their royal name. Ktima has interesting little museum containing objects that have been found all over Paphos district, and the Palace of the Metropolite has a Byzantine Museum with many interesting icons and liturgical vessels.

The historic site of old Paphos is about fifteen kilometres along the coast to the east of Ktima. Its modern name is Kouklia. It is one of the oldest Kingdoms of Cyprus, where we can see the remains of the Temple of Aphrodite. This was one of the most renowned places of pilgrimage of the ancient

Greek world, where thousands of people from all over the Mediterranean came every year to pay homage to the goddess. Nine kilometres further east is the legendary birthplace of the goddess, the place where she had stepped ashore, near a prominent group of rocks just off the coast known as the "Petra tou Romiou", where we can see the rich foam which no doubt bore some connection with the ancient legend about the foam-born goddess.

New Paphos was the seat of Roman proconsul, the Governor. His name was Sergius Paulus, an aristocrat from Rome. Pliny tells us that he was a highly educated person and a very important man. He was an authority in matters of physical sciences, open-minded, well disposed towards philosophy and theology; in short a sincere seeker of the thuth. His official duties, because he was the governor of a small territory, occupied little of his time. He was free, therefore, for spiritual work. As was customary for a Roman Proconsul he had around him a small court. Life in the province was rather monotonous, so the Proconsual had gathered around him worshippers of the Muses (that is of the nine goddesses who presided over literature and the arts and sciences), sages, poets, theosophists and other men of genius. Perhaps the most important of all them was a Jew called Bar-Jesus.

He was a theosophist or a magician. Romans were superstitious and would feel comforted having a man around who could speak to spirits and avert any bad influence on their masters. Bar-Jesus was a Jew, "Elymas", like the cynic philosophers who wandered around aimlessly (Elymas is the hellenized form of the Arabian word "Ulema", that means: wise). Elymas was a highly educated and cultured person, a theosophist, who knew well the Egyptian, Babylonian and Persian wisdom. It would be a mistake to underestimate his education, culture and capabilities. We should remember that this was the time when philosophers had become sophists and sophists had turned into magicians.

The teaching of the two Apostles had attracted the interest of many. The Roman Proconsul, hearing about the activities of the two men, invited them to his residence for a religious discussion and asked them to expound their doctrine to him.

Cyprus Famagusta: St. Nicolas Cathedral. →

Perhaps this was the first time that Christianity entered the high social class of the Roman aristocracy. Paul was very convincing. His ideas should have made a strong impression on the Proconsul. Sergius Paulus, as an intelligent man and a Roman lawyer, wanted to hear the other side *(Audiatur et altera parts)*, that is the views expressed by the Elymas Bar-Jesus. Then there started one of the most interesting spiritual duels in the history of the new religion. It was a dramatic duel between the kingdom of light and the kingdom of darkness. The Roman Governor was forced to realize that the religion of Jesus proclaimed by Paul was not simply another weak philosophical system, but the expression of power of the real God, that surpassed any magic.

Paul "filled with the Holy Spirit, looked intently at him" (i.e. Elymas) and said: *"you son of the devil, you enemy of all righteousness, full of all deceit and villany, will you not stop making crooked the straight paths of the Lord? And now, behold, the hand of the Lord is upon you, and you shall be blind and unable to see the sun for a time. Immediately mist and darkness fell upon him and he was astonished at the teaching of the Lord"*. (Acts 13, 9-12).

Paul won the day. The intelligent Proconsul was converted. His conversion was the first triumph of Christianity among the Roman aristocrasy and the ruling class. It is certain, that Christianity world have never conquered the ancient civilized world, if Christianity had not established its superiority over the magic and the occult religions. In those times, people would consider something as devine and true only if it could be verified by a miracle. This is why miracles are closely connected with all stories in the New Testament.

Elymas could not forget his total defeat. (About the whole journey to Cyprus see more in Acts 13,1 to 9 and 13). There is an old local tradition mentined also in official publications (Migne, Patrologia series graeca, vol. 86, 189), that Barnabas was killed by the Jews who were incited by Elymas himself. Mark, the nephew of Barnabas, buried the body of the Apostle in a Roman grave, near Salamis. It was at the time of the Byzantine Emperor Zeno (489) that the holy relics were discovered along with the manuscript of the Gospel according to Mark, that Mark himself, being its author, had put in the chest of Barnabas.

We do not know if the Roman Proconsul Sergius Paulus was baptized or not, but he believed in Christ. There was as yet no official Roman prejudice against a member of the Roman aristocracy, one of the ruling class, a Proconsul becoming a Christian. It was later that such a thing would mean death in the most brutal way.

The Apostles, perhaps, were obliged to depart at once from Paphos because of fear of retaliations by the Elymas, who exercised great influence on his followers. The most likely reason for the Apostles' departure was that they had spent much time in the island and they had to make haste so that they could pass Mount Taurus before the starting of the winter and the cold.

Paul never returned to Cyprus. He considered the church there to have been founded by Barnabas and that Cyprus wasBarnabas' field of missionary activity. Paul never wanted to build on the foundation laid by someone else. According to the Acts (13,13) *"Paul and his company set sail from Paphos, and came to Perge in Pamphylia"*.

It is not within the scope of this book to follow the Apostles in their journey on Asia Minor. However the journey to Cyprus and Asia Minor was very successful. The Apostles came back to Antioch with the trophies of their victories from seven strongholds that had joined the side of Christ: Salamis, Paphos, Perge, Antioch in Pisidia, Ikonium, Lystra and Derbe.

Paul in Greece

Paul was the Apostle of all nations. He was possessed by the thought of proclaiming the new religion in all the big commercial and urban centres of the Roman Empire. He was fascinated by Greece, the country of free spirit, the cradle of a civilisation which he had learned to respect and admire, the birth-place of the Language he had mastered in his early years.

It was early in the spring. March of AD 49. The Spring stirring of the year. Kings would march against their enemies. Merchants would travel abroad. Paul would feel the impulse that drove him away farther and farther westwards: Ephesus, Athens, Corinth, Rome. Rome was his final destination, but he kept it as a personal secret. The hellenising of the world had smoothed his way, but it was the public tranquillity the age enjoyed within the shelter of the vast, organised Roman Empire that made Paul's mission possible. A man like Paul, a proclaimer of a new religion would perhaps get into scrapes with local authorities, but generally speaking he would always be albe to move on, because the roads were open and the seaways free of pirates.

Rome was a firm ruler. When a breach of·the peace occured, order was at once restored. One could travel or trade from Mesopotamia and the Caspian Sea to Spain and the Atlantic Ocean, from Upper Egypt and Aswan to Britannia. There was a regional unity such as the world had never before known. Of this unity, this wide spread security, there was no greater beneficiary than the early church and its Apostles, the messengers of the new doctrine.

Over the wide horizons of the Roman Empire, Paul could open his wings and soar, like an eagle, over countries and cities without halt. Barnabas and Mark had already started for Cyprus. The time had some for Paul to move on westwards.

'And there arose a sharp contention, so that they separated from each other; Barnabas took Mark with him and sailed away to Cyprus, but Paul chose Silas and departed, being commended by the brethren to the grace of the Lord. And he went through Syria and Cilicia, strengthening the churches. And he came also to Derbe and to Lystra. A disciple was there, named Timothy, the son of a Jewish woman who was a believer; but his father was a Greek. He was well spoken of by the brethren at Lystra and Iconium. Paul wanted Timothy to accompany him; and he took him and circumcised him because fo the Jews that were in those places, for they all knew that his father was a Greek. As they went on their way through the cities, they delivered to them for observance the decisions which had been reached by the apostles and elders who were at Jerusalem. So the churches were strengthened in the faith, and they increased in numbers daily". (Acts 15,39 to 16,5).

Paul did not like to travel alone. He had two reasons. First, the order of the Lord that his disciples would travel in companion with another brother. Second, that he had "a thorn in the flesh", a mysterious and much annoying disease, that he called "a messanger of Satan", that was "buffeting him". It is probable that Paul was suffering from a bout of malaria, contracted originally in the marshes of Tarsus during his childhood there. Silas or Silvanus was for Paul a very good companion, devoted, reliable and generous in spirit, always ready for any sacrifice, his mind being broad and far from any Jewish narrow-mindedness.

Paul had behind him the experience of the apostolic assembly and the settling of the great problem of the new-born Christianity. It was the burning question that moved many hearts: How could one be a loyal Christian and at the sametime be a loyal Jew too? Or to put it in other words: Was it possible that one could be a Christian without first being intergrated into Jewry?

Paul understood the church as being universal. Paul had fought for the survival of the church. The danger that the early church would harden into a sect of Judaism and that Hellenistic Christianity would dissolve into a welter of non-historical mystery cults, had been averted once and for all as far as Paul and his mission was concerned.

This time Paul decided to travel by land. He was eager to visit his Asian congregations, the churches that he had founded. Walking along the old Roman road they reached Alexandreta, the city and the harbour which was founded by Alexander the Great, as the starting point of the long road to Mesopotamia.

It was here in this plain that the battle at Issus took place in which Alexander the Great defeated Darius, the king of Persia in 333 BC. It was here that then the destiny of Asia and Europe had been determined. Ever since, this decisive battle of Alexander the Great has attracted the imagination. Then it was that Hellenism, the rule of Hellas united with the East, was born. The barrier was broken and the two cultural tides of East and West met and mingled. Alexander the Great, the pioneer, was unknowingly the "prodrome', the forerunner, who prepared the way for the Christian message to the world.

Without the world expansion of the Greek language and of the Greek civilisation caused by this battle at Issus, the missionary journeys of Paul within the Roman Empire would not have been realized.

Paul, passing through the town of Lystra, took with him Timothy, the son of a well-established family of the higher social class whose mother was a Jew and whose father was a Greek. Timothy spoke and wrote Greek like a native. He became devoted to Paul and escorted him to Rome.

Here is Luka's narration in the Acts 16,6 to 8: *"And they went through the region of Phrygia and Galatia, having been forbidden by the Holy Spirit to speak the word in Asia. And when they had come opposite Mysia, they attempted to go into Bithynia, but the Spirit of Jesus did not allow them; so, passing by Mysia they went down to Troas".*

Paul was not attracted by the land but by the sea. There was something that always moved him towards the sea. It was perhaps that through the sea his ideas would travel faster and reach the commercial centres of Greece and Italy. So Paul headed for the sea and for Troy, passing the southern slopes of Mount Ida, the mountain of Gods from the summit of which (height 5.750 ft), as told by Homer, the Gods watched the battles of Troy.

The Vision at Troas

Paul and his travelling party arrived at Troas. It was there that the great Apostle beheld the vision which was mould not only his destiny but that of the western world as well. *"And a vision appeared to Paul in the night: a man of Macedonia was standing beseeching him and saying - Come over to Macedonia and help us-".* (Acts 16,9).

It was at Troas that Paul would see the European continent for the first time in his life. Europe's first island, Samothrace, could be seen at a distance, mistily emerging from the deep-water sea. To the north of Troas there were the remnants of Troy, the old city of Priam, founded around 3.000 BC and continuing, increasing or decreasing, for many centuries till the Hellenistic and Roman period. This was the city which was destroyed by the united Greeks after a ten year siege, the famous Trojan War.

In the same place Alexander the Great offered a sacrifice for the hero that he admired most, Achilles. Later in the same spot, his generals founded the city of Alexandria-Troas. In the year 189 BC the Romans established the "Ilium Novum", which was full of life till the time of Constantine the Great, who had considered making it the capital of his Empire. Troas was the place where Hellas and Rome shook hands. The remains of the Helleno-Roman city testify to this fact to-day.

Here the Greeks, more than a thousand years before Christ, had suffered much for the sake of a woman, Helen, the fairest in the world. Paul would easily understand the meaning of human grandeur and he would not pass there ghost-haunted places without emotion. Foremost in Paul's mind, however, would be one thing; to win the world for Christ. He had to run his marathon race and bring to the world the message of the victory of Christ. Nothing could stop him in proclaiming that the Son of God had defeated the Olympian Gods and that humanity's future was now a bright one. Paul would be very happy that here he could see his beloved sea. Universal sea and universal church, in Paul's thoughts would be united in one picture.

The travelling party of three, that is of Paul, Silas and Timothy, was met here by Luke, the physician, whom Paul had known in Antioch. Luke was the author of the third Gospel and the Acts of the Apostles. Greek was his mother tongue. This meeting was to have great bearing on Paul's itenerary.

Luke knew the sea well, a fact that makes us conclude that either he was born near the sea or that he had travelled a lot. It is known that Greek physicians were world travellers in those times. This simple meeting at Troas turned to become one of the most profound friendships in the history of Christianity. Luke accompanied Paul to Rome during his first and second imprisonments there.

According to an ancient introductory note to the third Gospel dating from the second century, Luke, after Paul's death in Rome, made a missionary journey to Greece, then known as Achaia, and died in Boetia at the age of 84 and was buried at Thebas.

According to another ancient tradition, Luke was a fine painter who had painted the icon of the Mother of the Lord. This tradition is also traced in the hymnology of the Orthodox Church. In the Acts of the Apostles, Luke however was master of the pen and not of the colours. That peaceful man was destined to become the biographer of the most vigorous man of the world.

We have two pictures full of life of the early church. The one was painted by Paul in his letters and expresses his zeal and passion for his mission. The other was painted by the quiet and steady hand of the physician, the surgeon, who could use the lancet and the pen with equal dexterity. One should not doubt that Luke, who had close connections with Macedonia, was the first to direct Paul's thoughts towards there. "Come over to Macedonia and help us" was the cry of Europe to Christianity.

Once there came from Macedonia that young hero twenty-two years old, Alexander the Great and brought to the Orient the gifts of the Occident, the Greek language and the Greek philosophy of life. Now the Occident was spiritually bunkrupt and begging, asked for the best gift of the East, the Christian message of salvation, the way of survival into eternity. "And when he (Paul) had seen the vision, immediately we sought to go into Macedonia, concluding that God had called us to preach the gospel to them" (Acts 16,10).

The Crossing from Asia to Europe

"Setting sail therefore from Troas, we made a direct voyage to Samothrace, and the following day to Neapolis..." (Acts 16,11).

The day that Paul and his travelling party, Silas, Luke and Timothy stepped on the Macedonian coast, marks a new beginning. Once brave and gentle people lived here, the people of the young king, who with his daring and valiant achievements made his people known all over the world and through

Samothrace: The "Winged Victory" of Samothrace now in the Louvre/Paris.

the centuries. But the time came when this young kng failed and his land and kingdom were taken over by the Romans. They, from 167 B.C. as new sovereigns of Macedonia, divided it into four administrative districts, the most important of which were Thessalonica and Philippi.

The sea voyage lasted only two days with an overnight stop at Samothrace. Samothrace is a beautiful island, with a European aspect, green and wooded. It has many natural beauties and it is rich in relics. The island lies in the northern Aegean and at a distance of thirty-eight miles from the mainland. It is mountainous and volcanic. Its highest mountain (1800 m.) is snow-capped almost all the year roud. It was from the summit of Samothrace that Poseidon, the god of the sea watched the battles of the Trojan War. The biggest centre of habitation was the town of Samothrace on the northern side of the island near modern Paleopolis.

The right of sanctuary prevailed on the island from antiquity. That means that it was a place of refuge or protection with immunity from punishment. In this asylum, at the beginning of the second century before Christ, king Ptolemy "The Physcon" took refuge, bringing with him all his treasures. The last king of Macedonia, Perseus II, did the same in 168 BC after his deafeat at the battle of Pydna, the ancient city in Macedonia. The island was occupied by the Romans. It was in the year 86 BC when the rich temples of the island were pillaged by pirates.

The ruins of the ancient city were first brought to light in 1863 by the Frenchman Champoiseau, who discovered the famous statue "Winged Victory", which was set on a ship's prow. It is now in the Louvre museum in Paris. This statue is one of the masterspieces of classical Greek art and is a testimony to the glory which this small Greek island enjoyed in antiquity.

Paul's party made a brief call at Samothrace, for one night only. We do not know where their ship landed since, as Pliny says, the island had no harbours. It is certain that Paul must have felt that he had entered a new world in the west, as indeed he had. The night that they spent at Samothrace led to the dawning of the brightest day in the history of civilisation in Europe.

In the evening of this historic day Paul landed at Neapolis, known today as Kavala. The modern city is a beautiful commercial and industrial centre. In the day large quantities of oil and natural gases have been discovered recently. The ancient name of the city has survived in the title of the local bishop, who is called the "Metropolite of Philippon and Neapoleos".

The city of Neapolis was founded by the Athenians in the middle of the fifth century before Christ and it is mentioned in history till Byzantine times. When Paul landed there, the visitor would be greeted from far away by the Temple of Artemis, in the harbour. The long "Via Egnatia", which linked the Adriatic and the Aegean Seas ended at Neapolis. It was his vital artery Paul had in mind, which was used as a Roman highway by all; merchants, officers of the army, administrators. It was wisdom which chose the direct path to the heart of Europe. Today a circle in the stone-paved yard of church of St Nicholas shows the lace where the party had landed.

Arrival at Philippi

Paul's travelling party after landing at Neapolis, moved "from there to Philippi, which is the leading city of the district of Macedonia, and a Roman colony. We remained in this city some days; and on the sabbath day went outside the gate to the riverside, where we supposed there was a place of prayer; and we sat down and spoke to the woman who had come together. One who heard us was a woman named Lydia, from the city of Thyatria, a seller of purple goods, who was a worshipper of God. The Lord opened her heart to give heed to what was said by Paul. And when she was baptized, with her household, she besought us, saying, "if you judged me to be faithful to the Lord, come to my house and stay". And she prevailed upon us. As we were going to the place of prayer, we were met by a slave girl who had a spirit of divination and brought her owners much gain by soothsaying. She followed Paul and us, crying, "these men are servants of the Most High God, who proclaim to you the way of salvation." And this she did for

71

many days. But Paul was annoyed, and turned and said to the spirit, "I charge you in the name of Jesus Christ to come out of her." And it came out that very hour. But when her owners saw that their hope of gain was gone, they seized Paul and Silas and dragged them into the market place before the rulers; and when they had brought them to the magistrates they said, "These men are Jews and they are disturbing our city. They advocate customs which it is not lawful for us Romans to accept or practice.

The crowd joined in attacking them; and the magistrates fore the garments off them and gave orders to beat them with rods. And when they had inflicted many blows upon them, they threw them into prison, charging the jailer to keep them safely. Having received this charge, he put them into the inner prison and fastened their feet in the stocks. But about midnight Paul and Silas were praying and singing hymns to God, and the prisoners were listening to them, and suddenly there was a great earthquake, so that the foundations of the prison were shaken; and immediately all the doors were opened and every one's fetters were unfastened. When the jailer woke and saw that the prison doors were open, he draw his sword and was about to kill himself, supposing that the prisoners had escaped. But Paul cried with a loud voice, "Do not harm yourself, for we are all here." And he called for lights and rushed in, and trembling with fear he fell down before Paul and Silas and brought them out out and said, "Men, what must I do to be saved?" And they said "Believe in the Lord Jesus, and you will be saved, you and your household!." And they spoke the word of the Lord to him and to all that were in his house. And he took them the same hour of the night, and washed their wounds, and he was baptised at once, with all his family. Then he brought them up into his house, and set food before them; and he rejoiced with all his household that he had believed in God." (Acts 16,12 to 34)

The city of Philippi was founded in 358 BC by king of Macedonia Philip II, father of Alexander the Great. In those days the neighbouring mountains and rivers were gold bearing. This cartainly attracted the founder's interest. He fortified the

Neapolis/Kavalla: The modern city of Kavalla (ancient Neapolis). It was here that St. Paul first set foot in Greece and Europe.

city and made it a very good base of military operations against Thrace. He utilized the gold that was washed down by the rivers and he built beautiful public buildings. The thriving city was occupied by the Romans in 168 BC. However, because of its location on the vital road artery, the Via Egnatia, it acqired new importance.

The remnants ofthe city were brought to light mostly by the French School of Archeology in Athens. We can see the city walls, the remains of a magnificent theatre and of a fine forum as well as the foundations of three great churches that had the arcitectural form of basilica. In ancient times and in the early church history a basilica was a rectangular building with a broad nave ending in an apse and flanked by colonnaded aisles. (The best restored basilica in Greece in the one of St Demetrios in Thessalonica.)

The city of Philippi became world famous because it was the scene of two battles (42 BC) in which Mark Antony and Octavius defeated Brutus and Cassius, the last of the Republicans. It was on the plain of Philippi that the imperial crown of the house of Augustus was consolidated. In gratitude he granted the privileges of a Roman colony to Philippi and its citizens did not pay any taxes. Generally speaking Philippi was a miniature of Rome. Philippi played a very important role for the future of both the Roman Empire and the Church. Along with the Roman veterans, there lived in the city the descendants of the Macedonians. Both were difficult to handle and to govern.

The Roman colonies were of various kinds and they served various aims. They were fortified positions within a residential area, or they collected food for the support of the poor of Rome or they were used as places of settlement for the veterans of the Roman armies. This third kind of a colony was developed greatly by the Roman Emperor Octavian Augustus (27 BC - 14 AD). Philippi was such a colony and most of its inhabitants were from Italy.

Here Paul found many women who followed him with enthusiasm. One should notice that in Greece the women were neither veiled nor segregated. When the new doctrine reached Europe it was the women who were converted first. Women played a very important role in the days of the early church. Women were those who had remained near the cross and attended the burial of the crucified. Women had the honour of finding the empty grave. In the terrible stories that one reads in the Gospels and which have to do with hypocrisy, hate, persecutions, abuse, fall and escape in fear, no woman is mentioned. There would never be a Christian Europe without the Christian woman at home as mother, wife or sister. Paul had a deep respect for the spiritually gifted woman. In Philippi, Lydia, a business woman from Thyatira of Asia Minor, trading in purple cloth, offered her heart to the new doctrine and her house became the centre of activity of the early christian community in the city. So the hearts of women were the seed-bed of the church in Europe.

Christianity does not need a suffragette movement since it offered from the very first moment of its establishment in Eu-

Kavalla: View of the city with the Roman aqueduct.

rope the right place to the women. The letter addressed by Paul to the Philippians betrays that the Apposttle had a soft spot in his heart for his first christian congregation in Europe. The letter is extemely cordial and friendly.

During the centuries that followed the church of Philippi some times flourished and some times declined. Its destiny followed the political movement of the region. The remnants of the city testify to its glorious and tragic past.

Two things the visitor should notice most: the ruins of the Byzantine basilica churches and the classical theatre of the city that has been restored and where perfomances take place every summer.

On the Way to Thessalonica

Philippi was the oniy city from which Paul departed not only with the approval of the local authorities but also escorted by a quard of honour. Paul, before he and Silas were beaten up and put in prison, had not mentioned that he and his friend were Roman citizens. He did it because he thought it proper for his mission. After a terrible experience in bleeding and in pain they were free to go.

The magistrates of the city had given the order for their release to the jailer. *"But Paul said to them. They have beaten us publicly, uncondemned, men who are Roman citizens, and have thrown us into prison; and do they now cast us out secretly? No! let them come themselves and take us out".* The police reported these words to the magistrates, who were afraid when they heard that they were Roman citizens; so they came and apologized to them. And they took them out and asked them to leave the city. *"So they went out of the prison, and visited Lydia; and when they had seen the brethren, they exhorted them and departed"* (Acts 16,37 to 40).

Beating a Roman citizen and putting him in prison before giving him the chance of a fair trial was illegal. According to "Lex Valeria" the magistrates of Philippi were guilty of a very serious violation of the Roman law. Paul knew it too. He thus had won the upper hand. After his departure the local authorities were very careful with Paul's followers.

Amphipolis and Apollonia

"Now when they had passed through Amphipolis and Apollonia, they came to Thessalonica, where there was a synagogue of the Jews" (Acts 17,1). It would be spring of the year AD 50 when Paul, Silas and Timothy started their journey towards Thessalonica, walking on the military road covered with granite stones, the Via Engatia. From Philippi to Amphipolis they needed two days, walking at least five hours each day. We would notice here that Luke had remained in Philippi to look after the affairs of the young church. He had not attracted the interest of the local authorities. The Apostles reached Amphipolis in the evening of the second day. They stopped to spend the night there.

Amphipolis was an ancient city of Macedonia, on the Strymon river near the sea and north east of Thessalonica. The place was known as Ennea Hodoi (nine ways) before it was settled, and was of interest because of the gold and silver and timber of Mt Pangaeon to which it gave access. The history of the city is connected with the history of the city of Athens. Amphipolis under Athenian administration became an Athenian colony, in the cause of which long fights were fought and important events took place.

Amphipolis was the Athens of Macedonia, since it had been for many years the centre of the brilliance of the Athenian form of government throughout Macedonia. The history of Amphipolis is divided into two periods, the pre-Athenian and the Athenian. The first is purely Macedonian; when the city was in obscurity and was named Ennea Hodoi. At that time, however, the city was fortified and a stonghold. It successfully resisted the attacks of the Athenians who, in 497 BC, under the leadership of Aristagoras from Miletus had come as near as the walls of the city.

Around the year 464 BC the Athenian colonists were driven away by Thracians, but an Athenian colony was finally established in 437 BC. This was captured by the Spartian troops and Brasidas and Cleon were both killed in a famous battle here in 422 BC. After the city was returned to Athens in 421 BC it had virtual independence until captured by Philip II of Macedonia in 357 BC. His retention of Amphipolis was a major cause of the war with the Athenians. The kings of Macedonia held the city until they were conquered by Rome in 168 BC.

It was from Amphipolis that Alexander the Great set out conquer the world. It was Amphipolis that became the headquarters of the Roman general Aemilius Paulus. He made it the capital of the Macedonian region. All through the Roman and Byzantine periods the city remained one of the most important cities of Macedonia because of its geographical position and its wealth. In AD 535 its name was Amphipos and Popylia and belonged to the second prefecture of the Byzantine Empire. After that the city gradually declined.

Amphipolis, because of its many adversities was not able to create a lasting civilization in works of art, as it could do in accordance with its temporal riches. As an Athenian colony, however, it was a centre of culture and the birthplace of many sages and scientists. All its classical grandeur is reflected today only on a few poor ruins mostly of walls and towers on the

77

top of the hill. We can see there the "Ilion of Amphipolis".

The Apostles spent the night at Amphipolis. Early in the morning they would have visited the town and realized that it could not become the centre of any serious missionary activity. They all had in mind Thessalonica, especially Paul, who preferred the large cities from where it was easy to disseminate missionary work to the smaller ones in the area.

They walked another two days, having on the one side the Gulf of Strymon and on the other the mountains. It was at the end of the second day that they arrived at the town of Apollonia, that had been named after Apollo, "the most Greek of all the gods", the god of light, in whom is no darkness at all, and so he is the god of Truth. Apollonia was used by the travelling party only as a staging post.

Apollonia was an ancient town of Macedonia that, according to Strabo, had been founded by king Phillip I of Macedonia at about the fifth century before Christ. It occupied a very important position situated on the Via Egnatia between Amphipolis and Thessalonia, about forty kilometres west of Amphipolis. The little town lived long and was destroyed by the barbarians in the fifth and sixth century A.D.

For the travelling party, the big city of Thessalonica was only twelve hours away on foot. It was late in the evening of the second day, or of the sixth day since they started from Philippi, that the Apostles reached Thessalonica, having in front of them the Thermaicos Gulf and at a distance the highest mountain in Greece, Mt Olympus (alt 2.918 m.), the home of Greek gods and goddesses.

Amphipolis: The Lion of Amphipolis

Thessalonica (*)

"Now when they had passed through Amphipolis and Apollonia, they came to Thessalonica, where there was a synagogue of the Jews. And Paul went in, as was his custom, and for three weeks he argued with them from the scriptures, explaining and proving that it was necessary for the Christ to suffer and to rise from the dead, and saying, "This Jesus, whom I proclaim to you, is the Christ." And some of them were persuaded, and joined Paul and Silas; as did a great many of the devout Greeks and not a few of the leading women. But the Jews were jealous, and taking some wicked fellows of the rabble, they gathered a crowd, set the city in an uproar, and attacked the house of Jason, seeking to bring them out to the people. And when they could not find them, they dragged Jason and some of the brethren before the city authorities, crying, "These men who have turned the world upside down have come here also, and Jason has received them; and they are all acting against the decrees of Caesar, saying that there is another king, Jesus." And the people and the city authorities were disturbed when they heard this. And when they had taken security from Jason and the rest, they let them go". (Acts 17,1 to 9).

Thessalonica was founded c. 315 BC by Cassander, king of Macedonia, on or near the site of the older Therma. He named the city in honour of his wife, who was a step-sister of Alexander the Great. Because of its geographical position the city grew up quickly. Its importance grew. Today Thessalonica is the second largest city of Greece, a major port, and an industrial and cultural centre. From the archeological view point the city, having been the second capital of the Byzantine Empire, is rich in monuments: -especially in Byzantine churches, notably Agia Sophia, with excellent mosaics, St. Demetrios and St. Georges. Striking amongst its ancient ruins is the triumphal arch of Galerius.

The rule of Macedon ended at the battle of Pydna (168 BC.), where the Romans, under Aemilius Paulus, defeated Perseus last king of the Macedonians. The city of Thessalonica became

(*) The modern city is called Thessaloniki, Salonica or Saloniki.
   Thessalonica: The "White Tower", the symbol of the modern city.

the capital of one of the four regions into which the Romans divided Macedonia (Macedonia Secunda). After the suppression of the liberating movement of Andriscus (145 BC), Thessalonica became the capital of the Roman province of Macedonia (Provinciae Macedoniae). Under Roman rule the city enjoyed great prosperity. Cicero stayed in the city in exile in 58 BC.

Philippi, city of veterans, had the atmosphere of militant Rome, while Thessalonica was a gay Greek merchant harbour. In Paul's time the city was not a Roman military colony like Corinth or Philippi, but enjoyed the privileges of a free city, being governed by seven magistrates (Polytarchs). They were responsible to the Roman Proconsul but they were elected by the people of the city.

Around the year AD 250 under the reign of emperor Decius, Thessalonica was turned into a proper Roman colony, an act aiming at latinising the city and its people. The opposite happened, as occured in other cities of Greece which had become Roman colonies. Instead of latinising the Greeks, the Latin inhabitants were hellenised.

The Roman ruler, Gaius Galerius Valerius Maximianus, made Thessalonica his seat around AD. 300 and built very imposing palaces. It was during the persecution of the Christians ordered by Galerius and his co-ruler Augustus DIocletian that St. Demetrius, protector of the city, died in AD 303. The emperor of the East Roman Empire, Constantin I, built a new harbour and Theodosios I fortified the city. During the Middle Ages Thessalonica was the second largest city of the Byzantine Empire and had an active cultural life.

Throughout its long history the city suffered many invasions. The Turks conquered the city in 1430. From then until its reconquest in 1912 by the Greek Army in the Balkan Wars, Thessalonica remained under Ottoman rule. The city had from early times a large Jewish colony which was greatly increased in the late 15th and early 16th century by the influx of Spanish-Jewish refugees. During its twenty three centuries, the city has always been an important centre of Hellenism.

Catacombs of St. Demetrius' church.

The "New Doctrine" offered to the Greeks

The Christian congregations of Macedonia were the Churches most devoted to Paul, their founded. It was them that Paul found understanding and spiritual comfort.

He wrote two letters to the Thessalonians. They are the first documents of Christian literature. In these letters he expresses his joy and satisfaction at the faith of the believers in Thessalonica and gives them some instructions on matters of faith and especially about Lord's second coming. From these letters (as from those to the Philippians, to the Corinthians as well as from his sermon on the Areopagus in Athens) we can learn what "the new doctrine" (Acts 17,20) was, which Paul offered to the Greeks, who proud of their culture, and fond of philosophy and science, nevertheless left all that to believe in the crucified Jesus. In his preaching Paul naturally emphasised these parts of the apostolic teaching and tradition which were most proper for the christianisation of Greek culture.

There were two main evils in the ancient civilization of the Greeks: idolatry and their anthropocentric ideas and tendencies. That is why Paul emphasised the living God and a christocentric life aboe all. The phrase "living God" meant for Paul that God is a personal being, always active in this world of time and space, though not confined within it, revealing himself through his actions towards men and his demands upon them.

All history is teleological, working one universal divine purpose: a process of redemption through Christ. The Holy Scriptures contain the wonderful actions of God, the story of how the salvation of manking was prepared and realised by Christ. The life of Christ, his death and resurrection were events, through which all the past came together: these events give meaning to all that happened before. Through them the course of human history was altered and a new manking came forth.

Christianity is a historical religion; it is founded upon certain historical events-the life, death and resurrection of Chrtist-which happened in the times of Paul under Pontius Pilate through the redemptive love of God. Those historical events were the main theme of the Epistles of Paul, while the minor theme was only the interpretation of their deeper meaning. This was Paul's gospel to the Greeks and their world.

The Escape to Veria (*)

"The brethen immediately sent Paul and Silas away by night to Beroa; and when they arrived they went into the Jewish synagogue. Now these Jews were more noble than those in Thessalonica, for they received the word with all eagerness, examining the scriptures daily to see if these things were so. Many of them therefore believed, with not a few Greek women of high standing as well as men. But when the Jews of Thessalonica learned that the word of God was proclaimed by Paul at Beroea also, they came there too, stirring up and inciting the crowds. Then the brethren immediately sent Paul off on his way to the sea, but Silas and Timothy remained there. Those who conducted Paul brought him as far as Athens; and receiving a command for Silas and Timothy to come to him as soon as possible, they departed". (Acts 17, 10 to 15).

Veria is an ancient city mentioned by Thucydides. According to tradition and Greek mythology it was founded by a daughter of Ocean and his wife Thetys. Ocean, a god of the waters, was a Titan, Lord of the river Ocean, a great river in Greek mythology which encircled the earth. His wife Thetys was a Titan too. The Oceanids, the nymphs of this great river, were their daughters.

The first known inhabitants of the city were Thraco-Phrygians. There were driven out by the Macedonians who held the city till 168 BC when it was conquered by the Romans. Under Roman rule Veria was a prosperous city since it was the first city to open its gates to Romans after the aforementioned decisive battle of Pydna. During the Middle Ages Veria was

(*) The modern city is called Veria or Veroia.
The ancient name was Berea or Beroea.

one of the most important cities of Macedonia dueto its geographical position on the left bank of the river Haliacmon, and its thriving trade. Throughout its long history it suffered invaders and conquerors. Finally Veria became free through its reconquest in 1912 by the Greek Army in the Balkan Wars. The city is famous for its many old churches of which at least twelve are Byzantine monuments with excellent paintings and precious treasures dated as far back as the 12th century A.D.

When Paul visited Veria it was a little country town. At this time emperor Claudius had ordered the explusion of all Jews from Rome and Italy. There was a danger that his decree could be applied to the Roman provinces as well. The Jews of Thessalonica had every reason to claim that they were loyal and devoted to the Roman emperor. To do so they accused Paul and his associates of acting against the decrees of Caesar by saying that "there is another king Jesus". The inmity of the Romans for the Jews could conveniently be turned against Paul and his followers. It was not difficult to succeed by bribery and by "taking some wicked fellows of the rabble, they gathered a crowd, set the city in an uproar and attacked the house of Jason, seeking to bring them out to the people". Their aim was obvious. Paul and Silas had to leave the town hearing the cries: "Paul Conspiracy! Treason against the emperor!".

Under cover of night Paul and his travelling party left the city of Thessalonica and walked along the shore of the Thermaicos Gulf. They left the Via Egnatia and, taking a country road, arrived the next day at the peaceful small town of Veria, the third administrative region of Macedonia. Paul intended to stay here for a while till things in Thessalonica became quieter. He tried twice to return but it was impossible because of the violent reaction of the Jews. He says explicitly in his first letter to the Thessalonians (2,18) *"because we wanted to come to you - I Paul once and twice - but Satan hindered us".* So Paul used his time in Veria to found a new church .

According to an ancient manuscript from the local Synagogue (perhaps of the second century A.D.) Paul remained in the city for a considerable time preaching and proclaiming his gospel. Paul's Bema is still there to be seen by the visitor. Near the steps from which Paul proclaimed his new doctrine we can visit a small monument enshrining a beautiful modern mosaic depicting the Apostle. This was built by the inhabitants of modern Veria in memory of Paul's ministry to their ancestors.

Luke, in the Acts (17,11) writes that the Jews in Veria *"were more noble than those in Thessalonica, for they received the word with an eagerness..."*. Here in Veria those who became Christians were many including people from the upper class and especially women. The number of women and their profound interest shows that we are in Europe, where women have a place in the family and in public life as well.

Paul in writing to the Philippians says that his enemies are like dogs. *"Look out for the dogs, look out for the evil-workers"* (Phil. 3,2). His joy in Veria did not last long. If one passes at night through a village the dogs of the village with their barking alert the dogs of the next hamlet so that they take over and escort the night visitor with their barking too. The same happened in Veria.

The Jews of Thessalonica came to Veria and stirred up more trouble. Paul had not other choice but to depart at once. The newly converted Christians escorted him to the nearest coast and put him on a boat sailing for Athens. Whether the ship sailed from Dium, the Roman colony Junia Diensis, at the foot of Mt. Olympus, is not certain. It is possible since the port of Dium was the nearest one from where a ship could sail directly to Athens.

Once again Paul's journeying ended in flight. Paul had made up his mind to leave Macedonia and to go somewhere else where the hate of his enemies could not reach him as easily as it did in Veria. However, Paul left in Veria a piece of his heart: Silas and Timothy. The newly born Church needed them there. They had to remain there for a while so that they continue the work started by Paul and interrupted by the malice of the people.

The Wonder that is called Athens

Paul travelling by sea arrived in Athens, the famous capital of Hellenism. Here in the Agora of the big city Paul met many interesting people, teachers and philosophers and spoke to them about the new doctrine of salvation. The philosophers found Paul's teaching of interest and asked him to deliver a speech on the Areopagus, the supreme court of Athens that supervised matters of religion and ethics of the city. The Athenians were surprised to hearing of the resurrection of the dead and about final judgement. The Epicurians were scandalised and mocked Paul. The Stoics told him that they would be glad to hear him again. Those who believed in Paul's doctrine were few, including Dionysios, a member of the Areopagus and a woman of noble origin called Damaris. Here is what had happened in detail, but before that let us have a brief resume on the history of the gracious and glorious city.

Athens more than any other Greek city-state was the hearthstone of golden period of ancient Greece. With reference to prehistory and history of Athens excavations have disclosed that Athens was first inhabited in the forth millenium by Pelasgians and later by Ionians. The first inhabitants found the towering rock a natural strongold and place of refuge in times of danger. Rising more than five hundred feet, this flat-topped rock was also the natural place for the palace of the kings. The days of rule by kings are barely recorder. When the nobles became stronger the kings lost their power and the Acropolis became the centre of the life for many, with temples and altars. Athens slowly climbed to the heights of civilisation, extending its influence over its neighbouring selfgoverned habitations and small villages, until these were finally persuaded to unite with the main city. Athens was an old city and proudly claimed that its inhabitants were autochthonous, had been there even before the settlements of Attica were molded into a single state. This union had been accomplished by Theseus. Thus Attica became the cradle of the Attic Civilisation. Trade flourished and this gave a start to the artistic development of architecture, painting and poetry. But Athens was soon to meet a serious challenge from both Sparta and Persia. Much smaller and less powerful than Sparta, Athens was more active and more effective in the fighting against Persia. The Persian armies invaded Greece from the north in 480 BC. After forcing the pass of Thermopile, they seized and burnt an evacuated Athens and then attacked the Greek fleet at Salamis. Here, the ships of Themistocles gained a sweeping victory and the Persians retreated back to Asia. The triumphant victory of the Athenians over Persia proved to the rest of the Hellenic world that Athens was powerful enough to keep its leading position among the Hellenes. In the years of peace that followed Persia's defeat, Athens enjoyed both prestige and power, and its only care then was to deck the city with ornaments in keeping with its leading position as head of all Greece. It was during this period that Athens became a centre of learning. Philosophers, poets and writers had leisure to reflect and to raise questions which were later to influence the whole of western civilisation.

Commerce continued to flourish despite the ravages of the Peloponnesian War (431-404 BC), but by the end of it, almost all that had been achieved during the Golden Age of Pericles was lying in ruins. The vitality of the Athenians however was great. Withing a short time they had revided their city, restored their fleet and were able to retake their leading position among the Greeks. The coming of the Macedonian conqueror, Philipp II to Greece, spelled Athen's political doom. The battle of Chaeronea (338 BC) reduced the city, and the Athenians did not dare dispute the mastery of Alexander the Great.

When Roman power was growing Athens became a rather inconsiderable ally of Rome. A period of stagnation was broken only when Athens unwisely chose to support Mithridates VI of Pontus against Rome. The result was the sack of Athens in 86 BC. During the Roman domination, Athens remained the cultural centre of the Roman empire, its "university city". It continued as a provincial capital under Byzantine rule and was a centre of religious learning. Athens (and the rest of Greece) remained under Ottoman occupation for almost four centuries. During this long period people suffered, but nothing could change their Hellenic character and orthodox religious belief. Athens was liberated in 1833 and was made the capital of independent Greece in 1834. At that time it was only a rather small village around the Acropolis. Athens grew swiftly after World War II. To-day the metropolitan area of greater Athens, with a population of more than two and a half million, is a modern city with a personality of its own; a curious blend of ancient monuments, Byzantine churches and contemporary architectural structures. The cultural legacy of ancient Athens to the world is really incalculable and Athens remains even today a cultural centre of world importance. In its universities and institutes of higher learning the student body is constituted of students from all over the world including "the black continent".

The ship that was bringing Paul from Macedonia to Athens sailed through the Thermaicos Gulf to the open sea till it reached the northern coast of the island of Evvia, then it turned right and entered the tranquil Evvoicos Gulf. Having, reached cape Sounion it turned right again taking its direct course through Saronicos Gulf towards Pireaus. At cape Sounion the stranger would have seen the Temple of Poseidon, the god ruler of the sea, the brother of Zeus and second only to him in eminence. The Greeks on both sides of the Aegean were seamen and the god of the sea was all-important to them. The temple is still there to be admired by those sailing by or visiting the Cape. This was the first salutation of Attica to Paul.

From his ship sailing along the coast of Attica on approaching Pireaus, Paul would see the Acropolis and the statue of Athena the Warrior, with her golden spear reflecting the rays of the sun. Athena was the daughter of Zeus alone, she was not born of woman, she just sprang from Zeus' head full-grown and in full armour. She was pre-eminently the goddess of the organised world, of the City, the protector of civilised life. Her father, Zeus, trusted her to carry the thunderbolt, his devastating armoury. She was one of the three virgin goddesses, the greatest, called Parthenos Athena, the "Maiden". The temple built in her honour was the Parthenon.

The view of the Acropolis and of Athena told the visitor that the power and the beauty, the ideals of human heart on this

earth, are gifts of God, inseparable from him. Separation from Him, who is the source of both beauty and power leads to the fall and to destruction. It was the threefold combination of religion, power and beauty that consituted the foundation of the glory of Greece. This incomprehensible wonder is unique in the history of humanity. A select few people reached, in less than one hundred years, -in science, in arts, in philosophy, in politics and in medicine the culmination of human genius. This wonder was called Athens, the city of Parthenos Athena, the goddess who is the embodiment of reason, purity, and wisdom.

The Greece visited by Paul was neither the proud Hellas of the Persian Wars and of Pericles, the country that loved its freedom; nor the united Hellas under the Macedonian rule, the country that could reflect something of the splendour and glory of Alexander the Great. After the fall of Corinth (146 BC), the county of myth and glorious achievement had been reduced to the status of a Roman province; Achaia, with decreased population, looted by greedy Roman public servants and deprived of the sources of its riches, was a mere shadow of Hellas. The country, towns and villages had been turned to ruin. Only Athens and Corinth avoided this fate. Athens owed its survival to the glory of its ancestors. Corinth had been revived from its ashes and had been rebuilt thanks to the needs of Rome.

Greece at that time was only a large museum of art for those who were visiting it. The Greeks were its guardians and the guides of the foreigners. Athens, however, in spite of all these, even at its lowest point of collapse, continued to exercise a fascination such that no Roman could think himself educated and cultured unless he had studied in Athens, while the Roman aristocracy considered a short stay in Athens a complement to their titles and positions. Men of letters like Virgil, Horatius, Cicero and Ovid found their greatest inspiration and their most profound impressions in the city of Athena, while politicians and men of power like Caesar, Antonius, Pompey and Augustus had expressed their respect for the beauty of Athens.

Athens: St. Paul would have entered Athens by the "Dipylon". View of the Acropolis and the Agora from the west side and the "Dipylon".

"Now while Paul was waiting for them at Athens, his spirit was provoked within him as he saw that the city was full of idols. So he argued in the synagogue with the Jews and the devout persons, and in the market place every day with those who chanced to be therel. Some also of the Epicurean and Stoic philosophers met him. And some said, "What would this babbler say?" Others said, "He seems to be a preacher of foreign divinities, because he preached Jesus and the resurrection." And they took hold of him and brought him to the Areopagus, saying, "May we know what this new teaching is which you present? For you bring some strange things to our ears; we wish to know therefore what these things mean." Now all the Athenians and the foreigners who lived there spent their time in nothing except telling or hearing something new" (Acts 17, 16 to 21).*

When Paul walked up the road that led from Piraeus to Athens, passed the Dipylon Gate and entered the city of Pallas Athena he had in front of him the miracle called the Parthenon. Even today there are only a handful of authentically great buildings in the world, but none of them approach the perfect dignity of the Parthenon, that utmost grandeur. Once it contained heaps of treasure from throughout the Greek world, and a stunningly elaborate statue of Athena which reached to the roof. Now we can see only the temple in its perfect nakedness. But depsite this, today we see the structure of the Parthenon very nearly as Paul saw it, even as the Greeks saw it when it was being built, when Ictinos was superintending the design and Phidias was carving the sculptures. It seemed at the time as if all the talents in the world had congregated in the city of Athens (about 440 B.C.) when Athens was hardly a city at all, but a huddle of small, low buildings at the foot of the Acropolis. Most of the Athenians lived in the Kerameikos, the beautiful suburb. Also in the area was the cemetery of Ancient Athens where Paul could see sculpured memorials and tombstones to illustrate his thoughts on the resurrection of men.

It is strange but true: the Athenians never succeeded in building a beautiful city with great colonnaded avenues like those at Alexandria and Antioch. They attached more importance to the intellect than to living-quarters, and more importance to the gods than to the people, they built their ideal city on the Acropolis for all to look at. They built a palace for the gods and were content to live in its shadow.

The Acropolis was not only the residence of Athena whose immense statue guarded the approaches to the sacred precincts. Acropolis was peopled by all the gods of Hellas. When the Romans conquered Greece, there was even an altar for Augustus Caesar. In Paul's time there was an altar devoted to the "unknown god". The Apostle worked this altar into the essence of his famous speech at the Areopagus. The inspired orator took as his starting point the inscription on the altar and produced his own teaching from it. The altar "τῶ αγνώστω θεῶ" and the inscription intended for pagan spirits were made through Paul's wisdom, istruments for the preaching of the true religion.

The city that Paul visited lay around the Acropolis, and most of the monuments of the classical period could then easily be reached on foot, as today. Today we can see the four remaining buildings on the Acropolis. All date from the period between 448-400 B.C. Paul saw the same buildings which made him think back to the days of the city's greatness, the days of glory and splendour. The Parthenon with its apparent simplicity of design conceals many architectural refinements. It was designed by Ictinus. In the early Christian era it was converted into a church. The Turks turned it into a mosque with a minaret striking out from the roof. During the Venetian siege of Athens in the seventeenth century, it was partially destroyed by the explosion of a cannon ball.

Paul also saw the Propylea, the imposing gateway to the Acropolis. The building has a central gateway and two wings, one of which was a gallery. It was built by Mnesicles as a processional entrance to the Acropolis. Paul would also have seen the Temple of Athena Nike, the delicate and graceful structure to the right of the Propylea, that is known as the "Temple of the Wingless Victory". The Athenias wanted their victory to stay permanently with their city, which is why their victory has no wings. The temple was built in the fifth century B.C. to commemorate the victories of the Greeks against the Persians. The fourth monument on the Acropolis is the Erechteum, the beautiful temple, Ionic in design.

Athens was full of munuments and statues, full of people who had come from all over the world. Paul, however, felt alone. He was lonely in the crowd. At the time in spite of all the activity, Athens had not a single leading personality. It was simply the "University" of the Empire. When Paul arrived, it was as if the history of the city had held its breath for a moment to hear what the "preacher of foreign divinities" had to say. God had given to the gifted Greek people the capacity to feel the divine in the form of the beautiful. Everything that remains on the Acropolis is a testimony to this fact. The Greek people touched the smooth marble with the fine and sensitive hand of its scluptors to see if it was possible to feel the beauty of God of Plato.

This ideal beauty of the Greek people was very high indeed, if we compare it to the ideal of the Egyptians and other people, who believed in gods, oxen fishes or creatures that were half human and half animal. The Greeks, unlike the Egyptians and the others, made their gods in their own image. Man in his harmonious form was to Greeks the finest revelation of God, an ideas that looks like a forerunner of the presentiment of the mystery of incarnation.

At the time of Paul's visit to Athens the worshipping of the Roman Emperor an accepted local religion. This continued for many years. Hadrian was the Roman Emperor (A.D. 76-138) who travelled much in the Empire and who was learned in Greek. He built in Athens the Arch of Hadrian and he completed the Temple of Olympian Zeus. In the temple there was the statue of Zeus made of gold and ivory and near it that of Hadrian's. The worshipping of both "gods" was equal.

All Greek cities had erected statues of Hadrian and proclaimed him god-saviour. Deification was the easiest way of an occupied country to express, or at least pretend to express, its gratitude to the conqueror. Whether it was genuine or not is another question. However, this is a classic example of servility and anthropo-worship going arm in arm. But the worship of God sets man free, while that of man enslaves him.

Panathenaea was a festival in honour of goddess Athena and in commemoration of the founding of Athens. Every four years the women of Athens embroidered a beautiful and expensive "peplos" for Athena, and the procession carrying the "peplos" to the Acropolis was the climax of the festival. It was in the Erechtheum and not in Parthenon, that the sacred robe of Athena was preserved. The festival included various competitions; gymnastic, musical, poetical and dramatic. We do not know if Paul had a chance to watch that festival. The whole procession of Panathenea would be seen on the famous frieze of Parthenon which Elgin later moved to London. Paul, with his scrutinising eye no doubt had seen it.

Paul would not have missed seeing the prison of Socrates, near the Acropolis, the wisest man of antiquity, the man who reached the limits of his knowledge. Socrates at the age of seventy was trying to bring his inner world always nearer and nearer, towards an existence which was entirely spirit, power and kindness. He belonged to the invisible, universal church of those who love God and seek the truth.

The fact that Socrates had found in his prison the strength to accept death as punishment for his ideas and convictions was something new, that never before had happened in Greece. It was like a prelude to the coming of Christianity, of the new doctrine that Paul had come to proclaim to the "violet-crowned and glistening city of Athens", as Pindar describes it.

At that time Athens was considered the religious, cultural and educational centre of the world. The Greek was a man who trusted his eyes. He adored the graceful and elegant line of human form, but Paul was looking for expression of the soul and there wasn't any.

After Socrates and the Orpheans, the Greeks, and especially the Stoics would see clearly that gods adored by the people were only indirect expressions of the one, vast unknown, the anonymous God. This was the God proclaimed by Plato, who used the inner world of our genius, and by Aristoteles, who, in his turn, used the external world, nature. But later on the Academy came with its prophetic doubt and the idea of "unknown God" disappeared again. Paul would see in the inscription on the altar of the "unknown God" the Greek sympathy for something superior to that which the Athenians had been taught to learn, a quest for the true God.

At Paul's time Athens was also the centre of mythology. Greeks had shaped their mythology-theogony with such genius and imagination, that the conception of gods by all civilised people had been formed according to the Greek prototype. The whole world constituted a unity, a spiritual universe where a graded hierarchy of personified divine powers prevailed. All these divine powers-gods had sprung from the supreme god, Zeus, who at the same time was the father of all gods and mortals*.

The Agora was the social and scientific centre of Athens. The civic life and most public buildings were concentrated within the Agora, while the Stoa, the market place, was filled with shops and administrative offices. Paul spoke and discussed his new doctrine at the Agora because the Athenians tended to spend most of their free time there. What Paul brought to the Athenians seemed to them a mixture of oriental nonsense. The Attic ironical spirit, mocking Paul, found at once a nickname for him "ο σπερμολόγος", "the babbler".

Paul's famous speech to the Athenians has been delivered to us through the centuries by Luke in the Acts of the Apostles. It does not matter if the text we possess is a short precis or a free account of the original speech. The important fact is that among scholars there is no doubt about the historical authenticity of this speech. The insignificant foreigner, the unknown Jew standing there in front of the wise and highly educated Athenians. It was only natural that the first meeting would end in conflict. The clash was between the rational and the metaphysical, between faith and knowledge.

So Paul, standing in the middle of the Areopagus, said:

"Men of Athens, I perceive that in every way you are very religious. For as I passed along, and observed the objects of your worship, I found also an altar with this inscription, "To the unknown god". What therefore you worship as unknown, this I proclaim to you. The God who made the world and everything in it, being Lord of heaven and earth, does not live in shrines made by man, nor is he served by human hands, as though he needed anything, since he himself gives to all men life and breath and everything. And he made from one every nation of men to live on all the face of the earth, having deter-

(*) You may read more on this subject in our next book for tourists and visitors to Greece: "Greece, the Country of Myth and Magic: Greek Mythology".

mined alloted periods and the boundaries of their habitation, that they should seek God, in the hope that they might feel after him and find him. Yet he is not far from each one of us, for in him we live and move and are; as even some of your poets have said, "for we are indeed his offspring." Being then God's offspring, we ought not to think that the Deity is like gold, or silver, or stone, a representation by the art and imagination of man. The times of ignorance God overlooked, but now he commands all men everywhere to repent, because he has fixed a day on which he will judge the world in righteousness by a man whom he has appointed and of this he had given assurance to all men by raising him from the dead". (Acts 17,22 to 31).

The Athenians asked Paul to appear in the Areopagus. The Areopagus lies west of the Acropolis. It is a small rocky hill on which the oldest Athenian council met. On the hill, cut into the rock, there were two seats, one for the prosecutor and the other for the defence councel. There was also, in between, a semicircular tribune for the judges, the members of the Areopagus. There were places for the public. Areopagus was the earliest Athenian council, highest and most respected. It was an aristocratic union, the classic court competent for matters of religion and ethics, for worship and for education. Areopagus and its members were greatly respected by all.

Paul's audience belonged to two philosophical groups, the Stoics and the Epicureans. We cannot easily judge the influence of the Stoa on the world's thought at that time. The Stoa was not something that had unity. There was the older, the middle and the new Stoa, the Greek and the Roman. The ethics of the Stoa were higher than its philosophy. What was the human element to whom Paul intended to reveal the Christian truth with comprehensive lucidity?

At the time of Paul's arrival in Athens most of the Athenians were men with confused ideas and inconstant principles. Doubt and hesitation prevailed on the thoughts of educated people. The old optimistic philosophical movements had degenerated to a simple believing in fate. Plato had stopped moving the minds of people and Aristoteles had ceased leading the way.

Only the Stoics and the Epicureans exercised a certain influence on the Athenian public. Paul had to preach to people with the most conflicting and contradictory ideas. The Athenians thought of themselves as being wise but in fact they were not. They discussed all things, the god and gods, the world and the worlds, about men and demons, but in the final analysis they denied everything except fate, they were agnostics and fatalists.

Almost half of Paul's audience thought in a Stoic way. The Stoic philosopher talks about god but he really means the university spirit that governs all, the immutable law or the mysterious secret power that gives to each existence the shape, the unity and the ability to act. Stoic was the first who put in ethical terms the idea of conscience. Menander was the one who said: *"For every human being, his conscience is his God".*

The other half of Paul's audience thought in an Epicurean way. The Epicureans did not believe in the gods, as many people did, but on the other hand they did not deny the existence of real gods. According to the Epicurean philosophy the world was the result of purely natural process with which gods had nothing to do. Gods, if they exist, are not concerned with man, therefore any concept of punishment is not acceptable. There is nothing beyond the grave. Man's goal was happiness in the form of unlimited pleasure. This philosophy of Epicureanism can be easily found in the modern meaning of the very word *"epicurean"*, that is the person fond of luxury and sensuous pleasure, especially eating and drinking.

Paul's God is not the God of only one nation or of only one people. The Olympian Zeus and the Pallas Athena love only the Greeks and despise all other peoples, considering them barbarians. Paul came and preached something entirely different. The unknown God to whom the Athenians made an altar and whom they worshipped, is the God who *"made from one every nation of men to live on all the face of the earth, having determined allotted periods and the boundaries of their habitation".* The people of the world may be divided according to their race, language, colour and other special characteristics but it is the spirit common to all them that unites them in one family. This spirit is the spark of divine nature that makes men *"seek God, in the hope that they might feel after him and find him".*

"Now when they heard of the resurrection of the dead, some

mocked; but other said, "We will hear you again about this." So Paul went out from among them. But some men joined him and believed, among them Dionysius the Areopagite and a woman named Damaris and others with them". (Acts 17,32 to 34). The Athenians, no doubt, hungered for life, but they accepted death with no hope of an after-life.

The Athenians became irritated at the very mention of the word *"resurrection"*. Some of them, the Epicureans, found Paul's ideas scandalous. He was forced, in view of the excitement, to stop his sermon because of the uproar and the protest. He did not even have the chance to mention the name of Jesus. It was very wise of him, however, to avoid doing so since he did not like to expose the holy name at the further expense of his precious mission. However there were some who wanted to hear more about the new doctrine. They told Paul that they would hear. *"again about this"*. This could mean two things, either a polite way to get rid of him or that they caught echoes of their own doctrine in what the Apostle had proclaimed. Paul obviously left his stand at the Areopagus disappointed. He expected more understanding. But his attempt was not in vain. Dionysius and Damaris *"and others with them"* believed. That was something.

The people of Athens did not care so much about truth, they only liked reasoning. Reflection for the sake of reflection was for them like a spiritual appetiser, a stimulant, that set them wandering in the labyrinth of thought. They had at their disposal the Greek language, the most refined instrument that people had never had. They had developed their talents of intellect to an incredible degree, but at the expense of the heart. They lacked the power of love and devotion. Idolatry went on in Athens for centuries. Four hundred and fifty years after Paul, Emperor Justinian I closed down the Philosophical School of Athens because idololatry was so persistent in the city.

The church that Paul established in Athens was very small. He never mentioned it in his letters. He did not write any Epistle to them. During his third missionary journey he avoids visiting Athens. The Athens' episode was a negative memory. Who could ever imagine that the new doctrine that Paul had proclaimed in Athens would be, in the centuries to come, the unique Palladium to which the Hellenes would owe the survival of their nation, of their philosophy, of their language, and of their very existence.

Paul's divine words echoed, however, from the Areopagus throughout Greece; the eloquent sermon on the divine religion of Jesus took root and expanded. The Greek Church fathers, relying on the teachings of Paul, combined wisdom with the words of the Nazarene and thus Christianity became an ecumenical religion, the root of true civilisation.

Corinth

"After this he left Athens and went to Corinth. And he found a Jew named Aquila, a native of Pontus, lately come from Italy with his wife Priscilla, because Claudius had commanded all the Jews to leave Rome. And he went to see them; and because he was of the same trade he stayed with them, and they worked, for by trade they were tentmakers. And he argued in the synagogue every sabbath, and persuaded Jews and Greeks. When Silas and Timothy arrived from Macedonia, Paul was occupied with preaching, testifying to the Jews that the Christ was Jesus. And when they opposed and reviled him, he shook out his garments and said to them, Your blood be upon your heads! I am innocent, From now on I will go to the Gentiles." And he left there and went to the house of a man named Titus Justus, a worshipper of God; his house was next door to the synagogue. Crispus, the ruler of the synagogue, believed in the Lord, together with all his household; and many of the Corinthians hearing Paul believed and were baptized. And the Lord said to Paul one night in a vision, "Do not be afraid, but speak and do not be silent; for I am with you, and no man shall attack you to harm you; for I have many people in this city". And he stayed a year and six months, teaching the word of God among them. But when Gallio was proconsul of Achaia, the Jews made a united attack upon Paul and brought him before the tribunal, saying, This man is persuading men to worship God contrary to the law. But when Paul was about to open his

Corinth: Remains and the "Bema".

mouth, Gallio said to the Jews, *"If it were a matter of wrongdoing or vicious crime, I should have reason to bear with you, O Jews; but since it is a matter of questions about words and names and your own law, see to it yourselves; I refuse to be a judge of these things. "And he drove them from the tribunal. And they all seized Sosthenes the ruler of the synagogue and beat him in front of the tribunal. But Gallio paid no attention to this."* (Acts 18, 1 to 17).

Paul left for Corinth realizing that his labours in the "violetcrowned" city of Pericles had been disappointing, but not entirely unfruitful. Paul in his first letter to the Corinthians (1 Cor. 2,3) in referring to his arrival in Corinth says" .... *I was with you in weakness and much fear and trembling"*. Paul felt that Athens, an entirely Greek city, with its pride in education, culture and the origin of its inhabitants could not become a base of operations for the cosmopolitan spirit of Christianity. Big cities were Paul's preference. He knew that here could fight his best. Thus he turned to another key city.

Corinth's two harbours gave it access to both Aegean and Adriatic. The harbour of Lechaion on the Corinthiacos Gulf afforded direct sea communications with the western world and its commercial, military and cultural centres, as did the harbour of Cenchreae to the Aegean sea and the east. If people heard something about Jesus in both harbours, its dissemination in neighbouring towns and islands would only be a matter of time.

The harbour of Lechaion, was not natural but man-made and cennected to the city of Corinth by long walls. It was the main naval base of the Corinthian navy for its activities in the west and the trading port for Italy and Sicily. The only public buildings mentioned here were the Temple of Poseidon and that of Olympian Zeus.

The harbour of Conchreae was on the Saronic Gulf. It was the port for Asia and the eastern Mediterranean countries. We have the information from Pausanias and from coins that, at the entry of the port, there was a statue of Poseidon holding a trident in one hand and in the other a dolphin. There was also the temple of Aphrodite and the ones of Aesculapius and of Isis.

Corinth: The Temple of Apollo.

Sailing round the Peloponnese was long, expensive and dangerous. So cargoes would be unloaded at the one end of the isthmus of Corinth, would be carried to the other end of it and reloaded in another ship. Small ships were dragged overland on rollers, or wagons or on sledges running in a marble tramway. One can see traces of it even today but only at the western end of the "diolkos", as this marble tramway was called. Many Corinthians earned their living by hauling ships over the isthmus. They pulled and dragged the ships over a low hill and down the other side.

The first man to think of making this marble tramway had thought also of cutting the Corinthian Canal. The technical difficulties were insuperable. There was also the superstition that Poseidon, the god to whom the isthmus was consecrated, would not like the cutting of his isthmus. The famous Isthmian games were celebrated in honour of Poseidon and took place every two years. In these games, like in those at Olympia, young men came from all over Greece. For centuries Greeks and Romans dreamed of immortalizing their names by cutting the canal. Periander (600 B.C.) seems to have been the first. Then followed Demetrius Poliorcetes, Julius Caesar, Caligula and Nero. Caesar, in preparing the invasion of Persia, sent his engineers to Corinth to plan the cutting of the canal to make his passing easier. Of the others, only Nero actively set to work and began digging. Nero even did some digging with his own hands. The governor of Achaia presented him with a golden spade and he dug up the first ceremonial spadeful of earth and carried it away. Nero had come to Corinth on the occasion of the Isthmian games. He seems to have remained for some days at Corinth watching his workmen digging. Among them were six thousand Jews sent by Vespasian from Jerusalem. The digging of the canal was stopped before Nero's assassination because he was a superstitious man. His engineers had told him that the surface of the Corinthian Gulf was higher than that of the Saronic. Many tried through the centuries to achieve the canal, but it was only in 1893 that the dream came true. Ever since small ships have passed through the canal which unites the Saronic Gulf with the Corinthian Gulf.

Corinth: The main street of the Agora with the Acrocorinth, the citadel of the city, rising 1.500 feet above sea level.

The modern city of Corinth is a few miles away from the canal and from the old city which was built at the foot of the Acrocorinth, the original citadel of the old city. Acrocorinth is about 1.500 feet high. The area suffers from earthquakes. The biggest occurred in 1928 when the city was destroyed entirely and had to be rebuilt. The old city was one of the most important cities of Greece due to its geographical position. It was of prime strategic and commercial importance.

Corinth played an important part in the history of Greece. There was a time when Corinth was the richest port of Greece if not of the whole eastern Mediterranean. It was the most populous city of ancient Greece, with the greatest wealth, the greatest number of warehouses, the biggest banks and the most courtesans. All the arts of luxury were cultivated there. Corinthwas the founding mother of colonies. The Corinthian coins, stamped with the winged horse, were second only to the coins of Athens in value. Over many years Corinth wallowed in the dullness of habitual prosperity. Corinthian luxury became proverbial "ού παντός πλείν ες Κόρινθον". Corinth rejoiced in the downfall of Athens and opened its arms to Alexander the Great, who proclaimed himself leader of the Greeks against the Persians, perhaps in the temple of Apollo.

There must have been at least two dozen temples in Corinth when it was at the height of its power, but today we can see only a few columns of the Temple of Apollo that survived. On the Acrocorinth, the great hill which rises above the city, there was once a temple of Aphrodite with its thousand courtesans where every sailor who entered the city paid tribute. Today we can see on the Acrocorinth the walls and a ruined Byzantine castle.

In 146 B. C. Lucius Mummius defeated the army of the Greeks, conquered the city and established the Roman province of Achaia. It was he and his army who killed all the male inhabitants of the city and threw all the women and children into slavery. This richest of Greek cities was looted by Roman soldiers and was set on fire. So the "Lumen totius Graeciae", the light of all Greece, as Cicero called Corinth was blown out. There was no Corinth; only the burning ruins of a

Corinth: Old and New Corinth seen from the height of the Acrocorinth.

fallen famous city. Corinth, proud as it was, suffered the fate of the proud. Perhaps it was the destiny of the city to be utterly destroyed. Inevitably Corinth grew rich from its commanding position; inevitably it gave way to luxury and thought itself impregnable; and just as inevitably it incurred the envy of all, especially of Athens and Rome.

Corinth remained in ruins for a century. Julius Caesar rebuilt it in 46 B.C. From that point on, in its coins and in inscrpiptions its name is *Colonia Julia Corinthus or Colonia Julia Corinthus Augusta*. The new city quickly became populous and prosperous. At the time of Paul it was the capital of Achaia, the province of central and southern Greece and the seat of the Roman Proconsul Lucius Junius Gallio. Before the end of the second century after Christ, Corinth became again the most beautiful city of Greece, exceeding Athens in riches and in importance, being the most thriving trade city of Achaia and its administrative centre.

In Corinth Paul met the Jewish-Christian couple Aquila and Priscilla. They were the victims of a decree issued by emperor Claudius in A.D. 49 according to which all Jews had to leave Rome and Italy. However, this order for the expulsion of the Jews was soon repealed. The couple were tentmakers like Paul. Paul lived and worked with them, prolonging his stay in Corinth for one and a half years. *"After this Paul stayed many days longer. And then took leave of the brethren and sailed for Syria, and with him Priscilla and Aquila"*(Acts 18,18).

In Corinth Paul founded the first church consisting entirely of Gentiles. He never accepted financial support from this church. He wrote two of his Epistles to the Corinthians. He visited the city more than once as we can conclude from Paul's writings (cf. 1 Corinthians 2,1; 12,14; and 13,1).

Paul wrote his letter to the Romans from Corinth during one of his visits there. In his Epistle to the Romans, Paul including in the list of the important people who sent their greetings to the Roman church the name of a certain Erastus, the city treasurer (see Rom. 16,23). The archeological excavations brought to light another important element testifying to Paul's sojourn in Corinth. There is a pavement block near the theatre on which can be read a latin inscription:

ERASTUS PRO AEDILITATE
S   P   STRAVIT

This means in English that "Erastus, in return for his aedilship, laid the paverment at his own expense". In the original Greek text of the letter Paul wrote

"ασπάζεται υμάς Έραστος,ο οικονόμος της πόλεως".

Οικονόμος της πόλεως meaning aedile, or edile, (from latin aedilis-building, temple). In Roman times the aedile was an official in charge of buildings, roads sanitation, public games etc. During your visit to Corinth, ask your guide to show you this important pavement inscription. Also you should see there among other very interesting things the "Bema", on which the Roman Proconsul would hold court and administer justice and which is located at the middle of the southern side of the Corinthian Agora, Don't miss it.

Other Places in Greece visited by St. Paul
Nicopolis (Action, near Preveza)

"When I send Artemas or Tychicus to you, do your best to come to me at Nicopolis, for I have decided to spend the winter there" (See Paul's letter to Titus 3,12).

Paul, writing to Titus, made a fixed appontment with Titus to meet the Apostle in Nicopolis, where Paul had decided to spend the last winter of his missionary life.

Nicopolis is a very old city of Western Greece, called also Actium or Action, near the modern city of Preveza (six kilometres away) on the Ionian coast. Nicopolis was founded in 30 B.C. by Octavian Augustus in remembrance of the victory of his forces over the naval and land forces of the Roman General Antony and his ally Cleopatra, the Queen of Egypt (31 B.C.). The battle established Octavian as ruler of

Rome. The city was known also for the Actian Games held there every four years.

Nicopolis had, in the days of Paul, a population of 300.000. The remains of the city are of great importance, especially the Basilica church of Bishop Dometios of the fifth or sixth century. The mosaic pavement of the narthex is decorated with one hundred and fifty mosaic portrayals, which constitute one of the best structures of the Greek old-Christian mosaic art, because they depict the whole creation of the world. Nearby, a second Basilica, the residence of the Bishop, the Metropolitan Palace, was discovered. According to an inscription on the mosaics, Bishop Alkysson was the founder. Today one can also see a wonderful theatre and the ruins of the temple of Ares (Mars) and of Poseidon. This temple was erected by the founder of the city Octavian Augustus in gratitude to the two gods, the one being the god of war and the other the god of the sea, who had helped the emperor in defeating his enemies as stated on an inscription found there.

Crete: Fair Havens and Gortys

"There the centurion found a ship of Alexandia sailing for Italy, and put us on board. We sailed slowly for a number of days, and arrived with difficulty off Cnidus, and as the wind did not allow us to go on, we sailed under the lee of Crete off Salmone. Coasting along it with difficulty, we came to a place called Fair Havens, near which was the city of Lasea." (Acts 27,6 to 8).

It was in A.D. 61 or 62 on his journey to Rome that Paul visited Crete for the first time. It was when he was taken prisoner to Rome to be tried as a Roman citizen before the emperor. The little port Fair Havens (Kaloi Limenes) has been known ever since as the place where the Apostle's life was saved.

This first accidental, visit was followed by Paul's missionary visit to Gortys, the capital of Crete, after his vindication and freedom. In the letter of Paul to Titus (1,5) we read: *"This is*

Gortys: The sixth century church of St. Titus, the first bishop of Crete.

why I left you in Crete, that you might amend what was defective and appoint elders in every city as I directed you".

Crete had made a strong impression on Paul during his first experience there, in spite of the hazardous circumstances. He found the island a good place for missionary work. The fact that he returned there having Titus with him proves it.

Crete has a glorious history of almost four thousand years. The excavations of Evans at Knossos unearthed a great civilisation, the Minoan, after Minos of the Greek myth. It was thus realised that some 3400 years ago in Crete men had learned to write, fashion exquisite jewelry, paint beautiful frescoes, control a complex society and rule the seas. The glittering Minoan culture was destined to end in about 1400 B.C. when a cataclysmic earthquake and 100-foot tidal waves caused by the eruption of the nearby volcanic island of Santorini, brought about the total ruin of Knossos and other Minoan cities.

During the Classical and Hellenistic periods very little was achieved in Crete, and by 100 B.C. the island had become a pirates' stronghold. From 66 B.C. to A.D. 395 it was occupied by the Romans, with Gortys the island capital. Gortys is 45 km. from Heraclion to the south or 34 km north of Fair Havens. Nearby you may see the sixth century church of St. Titus, the first bishop of Crete. Phaestos, famous for its Minoan ruins, is only 18 km from Gortys. The ruins of Knossos, of Phaestos and other small places, as that of Ayia Triada (4 km from Phaestos) are amongst the greatest wonders of the world.

When Paul visited Crete, Cretans had already a reputation originally expressed by the Cretan prophet Epimenides (sixth century B.C.). He said (and Paul repeats) that: *"Cretans are always liars, evil beasts, lazy gluttons"*. Paul further says that *"this testimony is true"* (cf. Epistle to Titus 1,12 to 13). As a result of trade and the influence of Egyptian and Asiatic civilisation, riches had made Cretans that way. However, Christianity had a profound influence on them. Cretans are today an inseparable and great part of the Greek people. Their continual battle for survival at the crossroads of history made them hard but brave. It was only in 1913 when at last their island achieved union with Greece. Today the Church of Crete is an independent Church under the direct jurisdiction of the Ecumenical Patriarchate.

Mytilene. Chios, Samos

"But going ahead to the ship, we set sail for Assos, intending to take Paul aboard there; for so he had arranged, intending himself to go by land. And when he met us at Assos, we took him on board and came to Mytilene. And sailing from there we came the following day opposite Chios; the next day we touched at Samos; and after remaining at Throggylium the day

after that we came to Miletus. For Paul had decided to sail past Ephesus, so that he might not have to spend time in Asia; for he was hastening to be at Jerusalem, if possible, on the day of Pentecost". (Acts 20, 13 to 16).

According to a reliable scholarly source* Easter of the year A.D. 58 was on the 28th of March. On the third day after Easter i.e. on the fourth of April, Paul's travelling party took leave of the Philippians.

At the harbour of Neapolis, modern city of Kavala, they found a small cargo ship that was sailing for Troas, for the little port of Assos. This small ship was the first Christian ship to carry pilgrims to Palestine and to Jerusalem.

In Assos they took Paul on board and continued their voyage. So they came to Mytilene-Lesbos, the island of Sappho, the woman poet, known for love lyrics who lived there c. 600 B.C. Having left Mytilene they did not land at Chios but passed opposite it. Chios was famous for the *"School of Homer"*, a rock plattform on which Homer is reputed to have sung and taught. It was the next day that they touched at Samos, the island where engineering achieved its first outstanding results, when Euphalinos built a tunnel through a mountain to bring water to the capital of the island. On Thursday, April the 20th, they came to Miletus. A few days later, on the 25th of April a fair wind brought them to Rhodes, the sunny island, where one can see the sun every day of the year.

Cos. Rhodes-Lindos

According to the Acts of the Apostles (21, 1: "....... we came by a straight course to Cos, and the next day to Rhodes, and from there to Patara"), Paul with his travelling party visited Cos as well as Rhodes, at Lindos.

Cos, in ancient times, was controlled in turn by Athens, Macedon, Syria and Egypt. During the Roman period it

---

* See more: F.K. Ginzel, Handbuch der mathematischen und technischen Chronologie, Leipzig 1914.

enjoyed great privileges. It was an important cultural centre and was the home of Hippocrates, the father of medical science.

Lindos was one of the three most important cities of the island of Rhodes. Cleombulus, one of the seven sages of Greece, was the Governor of the city c. the sixth century B.C. The city of Lindos helped greatly in 407 B.C. to found the city of Rhodes. Lindos kept its splendour during the early Christian centuries because of its trade, its riches and its naval power.

The Acropolis of Lindos, where there is a temple of Athena, is one of the most beautiful places in Greece. One should not miss Cos, Rhodes and especially Lindos. Nothing like the temple of Athena exists anywhere else in the country. The Acropolis of Athens is placed on the edge of a high cliff overlooking seas of the most superb blue colour. Paul entered the bay below the cliffs. On the cliff edge stands a ruined Byzantine church that was built in remembrance of the landing on the island of the Apostle of the nations.

Kos: The Temple of Asclepius (the god of healing) and the sacred forest behind. It was here that Hippocrates, the father of medical science, practiced medicine and where the doctor was regarded as a priest.

Epilogue

Paul visited most places in Greece more than once. He founded the churches in Macedonia and Achaia. He brought the message of God into the heart of Hellenism.

Hellas owes much to Paul.

Who could ever imagine that the doctrine which Paul had proclaimed in Greece would become the unique Palladium to which the Hellenes would owe the survival of their nation, of their language and of their very existence.

Greece is grateful to St. Paul for all that he did for her people and her future. The christianised Hellas became the cradle of a new civilisation that deeply influenced the future of the whole world.

Rhodes / Lindos: The day below the cliffs where St. Paul landed.

Page 118
Rhodes / Lindos: The Acropolis seen against the luminous sky, overlooking the dark blue seas.

Page 119
Rhodes / Lindos: The Temple of Athena on the cliffs. One of the most beautiful places in Greece.

TABLE OF CONTENTS

Page

PART THREE

TABLE OF PHOTOGRAPHS

Page

St. Paul's Journeys to Greece and Cyprus by Dr. Athan. DELICOSTOPOULOS

Cover: Front

St. Paul preaching to the Athenians. Famous painting (1867) by Ludwig Thiersch (1825-1909), now in the city Hall of Athens.

Cover: Back
The Areopagus, west of the Acropolis, the small rocky hill on which the oldest Athenian counciil.